Pero López de Ayala

Twayne's World Authors Series
Spanish Literature

Donald W. Bleznick, Editor
University of Cincinnati

Janet Pérez, Editor
Texas Tech University

TWAS 807

Coronica del Rey don enrrique repryo q asy ouo nonbn delos Reys q Regnaro en Castilla y en leon. q fue fyo del Rey don Jud C̃

Capitlo pmero Como los grãdes señores ot los priuados de los Regnos de castilla i de leon buxero al Rey don enrriq q quería mede tegnara ala villa de madrid C̃

Luego q se fopo la muepte del Rey don Juan fue tomado pn Rey enlos Regnos de Castilla/h

de leon y en todos los sus señorios su fyo el prinape don enrriq. q fue el tyxo Rey q asy ouo nonbn delos Reys q Regnaro en Castilla y en leon. Ot don lorey suays de figuepoa maestre de stntiago ot don goutalo tunes de gusman m̃. de calaquua luego q supiero la muepte del Rey priuepo de sus tiepas y bpnepo pa madrid y tpsapo al Rey don enrriq las manos pn su Rey ot pn su señor

A page from one of the Chronicle manuscripts.
From Manuscript J, British Library, ADD.17906.

Pero López de Ayala

By Constance L. Wilkins

Miami University

Twayne Publishers
A Division of G. K. Hall & Co. • Boston

Pero López de Ayala
Constance L. Wilkins

Copyright 1989 by G. K. Hall & Co.
All rights reserved.
Published by Twayne Publishers
A Division of G. K. Hall & Co.
70 Lincoln Street
Boston, Massachusetts 02111

Copyediting supervised by Barbara Sutton
Book production by Janet Zietowski
Book design by Barbara Anderson

Typeset in 11 pt. Garamond
by Williams Press, Inc., Albany, New York

Library of Congress Cataloging-in-Publication Data
Wilkins, Constance L. (Constance Lee)
     Pero López de Ayala / by Constance L. Wilkins.
        p.   cm.—(Twayne's world authors series ; TWAS 807. Spanish literature)
     Bibliography: p. 134
     Includes index.
     ISBN 0-8057-8247-8
     1. López de Ayala, Pero, 1332-1407—Criticism and interpretation.
I. Title. II. Series: Twayne's world authors series ; TWAS 807.
III. Series: Twayne's world authors series. Spanish literature.
PQ6412.L2Z97   1989
861'.1—dc19   88-25048

                                                                    CIP

For Heanon and John

Contents

About the Author

Constance Wilkins is a Professor in the Department of Spanish and Portuguese of Miami University in Oxford, Ohio, where she has taught since 1970. She received a B.A., summa cum laude, from the University of Massachusetts in Amherst and an M.A. and Ph.D. from the University of Wisconsin at Madison. She pursued her area of specialization, medieval Spanish literature, under the direction of the noted Hispanist Lloyd A. Kasten. Although Professor Wilkins has done studies on the prose of Gustavo Adolfo Bécquer, Golden Age Drama, and the position of women in fourteenth-century Spain, her major research effort has been concentrated on the works of Pero López de Ayala. In collaboration with Heanon Wilkins, she has published an edition of Ayala's *Chronicle of Pedro I,* consisting of a reading text, an extensive introduction, and detailed critical apparatus. She has received a number of awards, including most recently a Miami University Summer Research Appointment, a grant from the National Endowment for the Humanities, and a post-doctoral research grant from the United States–Spanish Joint Committee for Educational and Cultural Affairs under the Treaty of Friendship and Cooperation between the United States of America and Spain, all in support of the preparation of a critical edition of another of the Ayala chronicles, the *Chronicle of Enrique III.*

Preface

Pero López de Ayala is the most important Castilian writer of the second half of the fourteenth century. A study of his works must contain not only an analysis of the literary aspects of his prose and poetry, but it should also reflect his contribution as an historian. In addition to the general historical background of chapter 1, chapter 2 contains summaries of the chronicles, along with additional material. Although the discussion of each chronicle has been approached in a somewhat different manner, the information contained still reflects history according to Ayala—his selection of what he considered important or appropriate. Ayala's attitudes and philosophies, shaped by events that he observed or in which he participated, would be impossible to understand without knowing what occurred in his experience. Since the chronicles deal with the reigns of four individual kings, chapter 2 also makes possible a deeper understanding of the character of these rulers. This background also provides an essential framework for discussion of the chronicles as works of literature made up of some sections that can be classed as fiction and others that are nonfictional narratives.

This is the first comprehensive study in English of the chancellor's historical-literary production. In addition, the editions of the chronicles of Pedro I and Enrique III, prepared by Heanon M. Wilkins and myself, are the first modern editions of these lengthy and important prose works. In spite of the fact that there have been a number of recent editions of the *Rimado de Palacio,* very few studies have been done on the literary value of Ayala's prose or poetic compositions. For these reasons, the present study must be considered, in some respects, a preliminary one. Although I have tried to include all of Ayala's works, even those of doubtful attribution, it seemed appropriate to devote more time and space to the chronicles. Their value and interest is widely acknowledged, but their extraordinary length has kept them from being read carefully and in their entirety. Ayala's skill as a prose stylist has received little attention.

One of the important goals of this study, therefore, is to acquaint the reader with these works and to stimulate greater interest in them. As the bibliography reveals, most of the studies of the *Rimado* deal with sources, chronology, or structure. Articles dealing with literary techniques and devices, or with Ayala's original contribution to the poetic rendition of his sources are rare. This study has the aim of encouraging further consideration of this important author.

I wish to express my appreciation to my husband, Heanon M. Wilkins, for without his constant encouragement, this book would not have been written; to Miami University for a year-long Faculty Improvement Leave 1978–79; and, finally, to Betty Marak for her skill and patience in typing the manuscript.

Constance L. Wilkins

Miami University, Oxford, Ohio

Chronology

1304   The Frenchman Clement V is elected pope. Papacy moved to Avignon in 1307.

1332   Coronation of Alfonso XI. Pero López de Ayala born in Alava.

1333   Armies from Granada and Morocco reconquer Gibraltar.

1337   Beginning of Hundred Years' War between France and England.

1340   Alfonso XI conquers Muslims at the Battle of Salado.

1342   Alfonso XI initiates the *alcabala,* a new royal tax on commercial transactions.

1343   Pere IV of Aragon annexes the Balearic Islands.

1344   Alfonso XI conquers Algeciras.

1347   English take Calais. Rebellion of the Aragonese and Valentian nobility against Pere "the Ceremonious."

1348   In the Cortes in Alcalá de Henares, Alfonso XI reorganizes the administration of justice. The *Siete Partidas* of Alfonso X are recognized as the law of the land. Black Death strikes Spain and the rest of Europe.

1350   Alfonso XI dies during the siege of Gibraltar; sixteen-year-old Pedro I assumes the throne.

1353   Rebellion of nobles against Pedro I; nobles led by Enrique of Trastámara are defeated and take refuge in France. Ayala serves as page to Pedro I of Castile.

1354   Ayala serves as page to the Infante Fernando of Aragon.

1356   Beginning of the Castilian-Aragonese war, also known as the war of the two Pedros; it marks the beginning of Castilian hegemony.

1359   Ayala commands one of the ships of Pedro I in the battle against Aragon.

1360   French and English sign Treaty of Brittany. Edward III renounces his claim to the French throne. Ayala becomes chief constable of Toledo.

1366   Enrique of Trastámara proclaims himself King of Castile after having invaded Castile with the help of Bertrand Du Guesclin and the "white companies."

1367   Ayala joins Enrique of Trastámara in the Battle of Nájera against the forces of Pedro I and his English allies. Enrique is defeated. Ayala is taken prisoner by the English.

1369   Pedro I assassinated in Montiel; Enrique II becomes king of Castile.

1371   John of Gaunt, duke of Lancaster, marries daughter of Pedro I and lays claim to the throne of Castile. Ayala appointed chief standard bearer.

1372   French, aided by Castile, defeat the English fleet in Rochelle.

1374   Ayala appointed mayor and chief judge of the sheep trails of Vitoria.

1375   Ayala becomes mayor of Toledo.

1376   Ayala represents Enrique II in the court of Pere IV of Aragon.

1378   Pope Gregory IX dies; beginning of papal schism: Urbano VI in Rome and Clement VII in Avignon. Ayala serves as ambassador of Castile in the court of Charles V of France.

1379   Enrique II dies, Juan I accedes to the throne. Ayala represents Castile in Paris in the talks to renew the alliance between Castile and France.

1382   Juan I sends Ayala to assist and counsel the king of France in the Battle of Rosebeck.

1384   Master of Avis is proclaimed king of Portugal. Ayala serves as ambassador in the papal court at Avignon.

1385   Ayala participates in talks with the high constable of Portugal in an attempt to bring about a reconciliation between Castile and Portugal. The Portuguese defeat the Castilians at Aljubarrota. Ayala imprisoned for more than two years in Portugal.

1386   *Libro de la caça de las aves* completed.

1388–1389   Ayala represents Juan I in Bayonne to sign the agreement in which the duke of Lancaster gives up all claims to Castilian throne. Treaty signed with Portugal.

1390 Juan I of Castile dies; Enrique III becomes king. Ayala participates in discussions concerning the regency.

1391 Unrest in Castile because of problems during the minority of Enrique III. Anti-Semitic propaganda results in widespread pogroms in Spain.

1393 Enrique III proclaimed of legal age. Ayala serves as a negotiator to renew the treaty between Castile and Portugal.

1394 Death of Pope Clement VII in Avignon; Pedro de Luna, cardinal from Aragon, elected Pope Benedict XIII.

1395 Ayala is present in Avignon during the dramatic conflict between Pope Benedict XIII and the French dukes and cardinals.

1396 Ayala attends the meeting in which Richard II of England and Charles VI of France attempt to draw up peace treaties.

1399 Ayala appointed grand chancellor of Castile.

1404 Ayala completes *Rimado de Palacio.*

1405 Future Juan II of Castile is born.

1406 Enrique III of Castile dies.

1407 Ayala dies in Calahorra.

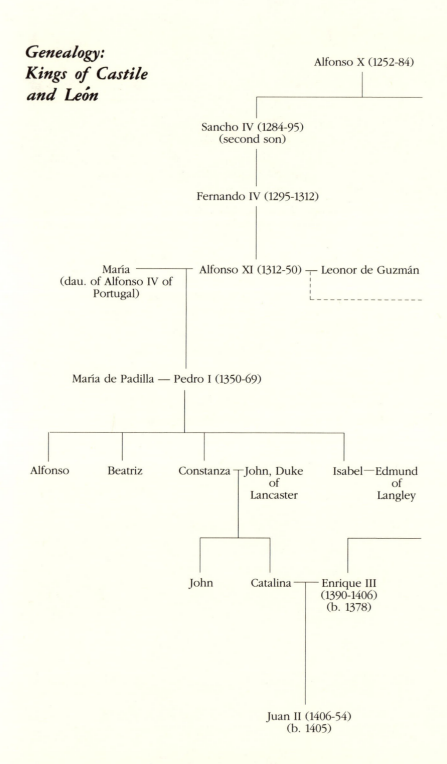

**Genealogy:
Kings of Castile
and León**

Alfonso X (1252-84)

Sancho IV (1284-95)
(second son)

Fernando IV (1295-1312)

María ——————— Alfonso XI (1312-50) —— Leonor de Guzmán
(dau. of Alfonso IV of
Portugal)

María de Padilla — Pedro I (1350-69)

Alfonso   Beatriz   Constanza —┬— John, Duke   Isabel—Edmund
                                    of   of
                                 Lancaster   Langley

John   Catalina —┬— Enrique III
                      (1390-1406)
                      (b. 1378)

Juan II (1406-54)
(b. 1405)

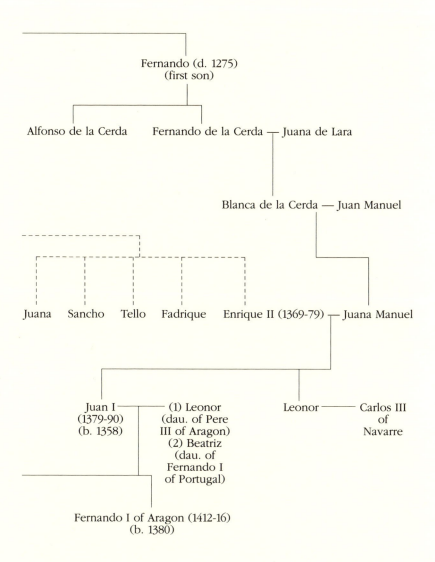

Fernando (d. 1275)
(first son)

Alfonso de la Cerda

Fernando de la Cerda — Juana de Lara

Blanca de la Cerda — Juan Manuel

Juana   Sancho   Tello   Fadrique   Enrique II (1369-79) — Juana Manuel

Juan I   (1) Leonor   Leonor ———— Carlos III
(1379-90)   (dau. of Pere   of
(b. 1358)   III of Aragon)   Navarre
                    (2) Beatriz
                    (dau. of
                    Fernando I
                    of Portugal)

Fernando I of Aragon (1412-16)
(b. 1380)

Chapter One

The Life and Times of Pero López de Ayala

A World in Ferment

Pero López de Ayala, chronicler, poet, and statesman, lived from 1332 to 1407, a period spanning the reigns of five Castilian kings. During this epoch, all of Western Europe, including the Iberian Peninsula, experienced a series of transformations that have been likened to a state of fermentation.[1] Fourteenth-century Spain, especially Castile, witnessed a surprising succession of events that decisively shaped its economic, social, and political history. By the time of Ayala's birth the long minority of Alfonso XI had ended, and the kingdom was beginning to recover from the divisive and debilitating effects of the tutorial government and the economic recession. Several years of adverse weather conditions had caused a reduction in cattle and a scarcity of crops. Many Castilian towns were left virtually uninhabited as farm workers migrated farther south to Andalusia to cultivate unappropriated land that was nearly rent and tax free. The dissension between the tutors resulted in political instability and encouraged rampant disorder throughout the land.

During his reign, Alfonso XI was able to diminish the power of the nobility, using a variety of means ranging from assassination to pardon, and he succeeded in reestablishing a strong monarchy. By maintaining Castile's neutrality in the conflict between France and England, he was able to concentrate his military force against the Moors. His victory in the battle of Salado ended the last threat of Muslim invasion across the Strait of Gibraltar, and the conquest of Algeciras meant relative control over the Straits. Some historians, for example, Luis Suárez Fernández, believe that had he lived longer, Alfonso XI would have completely expelled the Moors from the Iberian Peninsula. The Castilian monarchs of the remainder of the fourteenth century were not able to devote their energies to the Reconquest, preferring in general to maintain a truce with Granada. By doing this, they freed their military and economic resources to deal with more pressing problems.

Who Pays for the Plague?

Around mid-century, Spain and other European countries were beset by plagues and epidemics, which in some areas claimed from one fourth to one half of the population. Many persons attributed the plague, hunger, and epidemics to divine punishment, and in extreme cases penitents atoned for their sins by self-flagellation. Some religious zealots victimized Jews, blaming them for the hardships and bad times. In the course of a long history of anti-Semitism, the Jews had been expelled from France, England, and other countries. Castile, however, was a relatively hospitable land, increasing its Semitic population through reconquest of southern territories and by allowing Jews expelled or persecuted in other lands to settle there.

For the most part, the situation remained favorable during the reigns of Alfonso XI and Pedro I, when administrative and intellectual activities of the Jews were encouraged. Although subject to Christian authorities, the Spanish Jews lived in their own communities and paid taxes directly to the monarchs, who were in turn responsible for their protection. Some evidence of change is seen as early as the end of Alfonso's reign when laws were introduced forbidding Jews and Muslims to lend money or to act as tax farmers. Pedro I was accused by his enemies of treating the Jews too favorably and including too many in high government posts, even though his treasurer Samuel Levi was put to death, presumably at the king's orders. Despite the fact that Enrique II continued to use Jews in administrative positions, Jewish quarters were sacked or heavy taxes were levied to finance his army, and laws were passed mandating the wearing of distinctive clothing. Periodic flare-ups of anti-Jewish sentiment were kept under control by the crown for most of the second half of the century, until the lack of centralized control permitted the mounting tension between Christians and Jews to erupt in the form of the vicious and bloody pogroms of 1391.

A New Dynasty and World Problems

Castile's involvement in two of the most important historical events of this era, the Hundred Years' War and the Great Schism, is directly related to the dynastic struggle that began when Enrique, the illegitimate son of Alfonso XI, tried to wrest the throne from the legitimate monarch, Pedro I. The English lent aid to Pedro, while Enrique's invasion of Castile was supported by French troops. The war between England and France lasted from 1337 to 1453 and eventually involved nearly all of Western Europe. The dispute began in 1328 when Charles IV of France died without a male heir. The throne was claimed by both Edward III of England and Felipe of Valois. France in the first half of the fourteenth century was the most powerful, largest, richest, and most populous state in Europe. England was the most likely rival. The war was prolonged by disputes over English territorial possessions in France, by commercial rivalry, and by greed for plunder. On land the war was fought mainly in France, while the Gulf of Vizcaya was the site of most naval activity. The Castilian civil war gave the future constable of France, Bertrand Du Guesclin, the opportunity to gain field experience for his companies. The French also reaped great benefits from this investment in the form of naval support from the ever-more powerful Castilian fleet. Castilian ships sacked English coastal towns and participated in the decisive battle of Rochelle in 1372.

The Castilian-French alliance was faithfully maintained by the first three monarchs of the new Trastamaran dynasty, a fact that also accounts for Castile's advocacy of the Avignon pope during the Great Schism. Although the popes had resided in Avignon for a number of years, Gregory XI happened to die in Rome in 1378. It is possible that public agitation influenced the election of the new pope, Urban VI. Urban VI immediately antagonized the cardinals, ten of whom were French. In another election, they selected Roberto of Geneva as Pope Clement VII. The second pope returned to the papal residence at Avignon. Both popes were convinced of their own right, and the European countries pledged obedience to one or the other along political lines. The schism lasted nearly forty years and resulted in a grave problem of authority, moral crises, and disciplinary disorder. The church never decided which of the two was right, although tradition has always been hostile to the Avignon popes. Although Castile and England were on opposite sides in this dispute, the schism was more or less ignored when a marriage was arranged between the son and heir of Juan I of Castile and Catalina, daughter of the duke of Lancaster and granddaughter of Pedro I. This arrangement finally resolved the dynastic discord, and the Castilian-English antagonism was diminished.

In spite of the civil war and the wars with Aragon and Portugal in the second half of the fourteenth century, Castile made advances in industry and commerce, becoming one of the leading naval powers in Europe and one of the chief producers and exporters of raw wool. Although still mainly an agricultural country, urban centers became more densely populated, and the cities at times were able to exercise considerable influence on governmental decisions. The problem of the conflict between the monarchy and the nobility during this period is complicated by the fact that power and influence among the nobles shifted from one group to another. A powerful noble class was encouraged and promoted by Enrique II in order to undermine Pedro I, and was relied upon by Juan I for advice in his council and in the Cortes. During the youth of Enrique III, the lower nobility succeeded in ousting the members of the king's family and concentrating wealth and influence in their own hands.

Pero López de Ayala: The Early Years

Pero López de Ayala figured as a prominent member of this new group of influential nobles. Although there is relatively little information concerning Ayala's youth, his life as a politician and writer is better known than that of many other writers before, contemporary, or even after him.[2] Born in the northern province of Alava, he was the son of Don Fernán Pérez de Ayala and Doña Elvira Alvarez de Ceballos. Fernán Pérez was a rather wealthy nobleman who held important posts during the reigns of Alfonso XI and Pedro I. Doña Elvira, who came from the region of the Montaña, was a rich noblewoman whose inheritance provided a large increment to the family wealth.[3] It is believed that Ayala's uncle, Cardinal Pedro Gómez Barroso, raised and educated him and must have had a great influence on him.[4] Ayala's knowledge of Latin and French, and his interest in the Bible and other religious writings undoubtedly had their origins in this early ecclesiastical training. At the age of twenty-one, he entered the service of Pedro I.

Activities at Court

Much of what is known of Ayala's activities, especially during the years of Pedro's rule, is derived from the chronicles he wrote describing the reigns of Pedro I (1350–69), Enrique II (1369–79), Juan I (1379–90), and Enrique III (1390–1406). Ayala first appears in the *Corónica del rey don Pedro* as a page who is selected to carry the king's banner. This event occurred in 1353—the same year in which Ayala attended the marriage of Pedro and Doña Blanca de Borbón. In 1359 he is listed as captain of one of the ships Pedro sent against Aragon, and two years later he appears as chief constable of Toledo. In the latter post, Ayala was given the questionable honor of guarding the archbishop of Toledo prior to the latter's exile to Portugal. Although he had been insulted by the king's messenger and believed in the archbishop's innocence, Ayala adhered firmly to his duty to obey his king's orders. In fact, Ayala remained loyal to Pedro longer than many of the other nobles, even following him as he fled south, leaving the people of Burgos defenseless. By 1367, however, he had joined Enrique of Trastámara and shortly afterward was taken prisoner by the English during the Battle of Nájera.

During the reign of Enrique II, Ayala was the recipient of many royal favors, including territorial possessions and the important posts of chief judge of sheep trails of Vitoria and Mayor of Toledo. His political activity greatly increased during the reign of Juan I when he served as royal counselor and as ambassador to France. In appreciation for his military advice, Charles VI of France granted him a generous annual pension to be received during Ayala's lifetime and that of his eldest son. In his position of royal advisor, Ayala attempted to preserve the peace between Castile and Portugal and opposed the plan of Juan I to assume the Portuguese throne and thereby unite the two kingdoms. Unfortunately, Ayala failed in his efforts. He participated in the disastrous Battle of Aljubarrota where he was taken captive by the Portuguese and imprisoned for two years. It is probable that some of his writings were done during this period, especially the *Libro de la caza de las aves* (Book of falconry) and some poetic works. After he was freed, Ayala continued his active participation in the affairs of the government. He was one of the royal messengers sent to Bayonne to negotiate with the duke of Lancaster the arrangements and conditions of the wedding of the latter's daughter Catalina and the Infante Enrique. Perhaps one of Ayala's most important actions took place in the last year of the reign of Juan I. The king had not given up his aspirations to the throne of Portugal and, in an effort to make his sovereignty more acceptable to the Portuguese people, he planned to divide his kingdom, giving Castile and León to his eldest son Enrique. In a reasoned, persuasive speech before the Cortes of Guadalajara, the royal council with a single voice convinced the reluctant king to abandon his plan to renounce the throne of Castile.

Ayala's importance and influence in the kingdom continued to increase during the reign of Enrique III. He was a member of the Council of Regents during Enrique's minority and served as a negotiator in the peace talks with Portugal. After the young king assumed personal control of the government in 1393, Ayala was able to spend several years in semiretirement at his estate in Alava and at the adjacent Hieronymite monastery of San Miguel del Monte. He had contributed generously to the financing of the monastery when it was founded, and continued to be one of its patrons. It is believed that he wrote his chronicles and the *Libro del linaje de Ayala* (Book of the lineage of Ayala) during these peaceful sojourns away from the affairs of state. In 1399, the greatest honor was bestowed on the venerable statesman when Enrique III appointed him grand chancellor of the kingdom.

A Fifteenth-Century Portrait

The literary portrait of Ayala by his nephew Fernán Pérez de Guzmán in *Generaciones y semblanzas* describes the chancellor this way:

This Pero López de Ayala was tall and slender and a good person, a man of great discretion and authority and of great counsel both in times of peace and of war. He had a close association with the kings during whose reigns he lived, for when he was a youth he was well liked by King Pedro and afterwards by King Enrique II. He was in his council and was greatly loved by him. King Juan and King Enrique, his son, honored him and had great confidence in him. He experienced many events in both war and peace. He was captured twice, once in the Battle of Nájera and another time in Aljubarrota.

He had a pleasing personality and was an interesting conversationalist. He was conscientious and very God-fearing. He loved knowledge very much and devoted himself a great deal to books and histories. In spite of the fact that he was by all standards an excellent knight and showed great prudence in secular discourse, he was by nature very inclined to the sciences and because of this he spent a great deal of his time reading and studying, not works of law but rather moral philosophy and histories. Because of him, some books are known in Castile which were unknown before. . . .[5]

Ayala the Writer

In addition to being an impressive political and military leader who was personally acquainted with popes and kings, Ayala also must be acknowledged as one of the three major literary figures of his century. In contrast to the many literary works of the earlier Middle Ages whose authors remain anonymous, the first half of the fourteenth century is dominated by the forceful personalities of Don Juan Manuel and Juan Ruiz, archpriest of Hita. All three writers in their own way reflect the social, economic, and political milieu in which they lived, as well as their own personal reactions to their circumstances. Although a self-consciousness as literary creators is apparent in the work of each of these authors, their primary purpose remains didactic—ranging from the jocular tongue-in-cheek admonitions of Juan Ruiz to the chivalric preoccupations and moralizing of Juan Manuel and the almost ascetic severity of Pero López. As the most important writer of the last half of the century, Ayala's prose and poetic works are significant for a number of reasons. Linguistically, they comprise an extensive and reliable source of late fourteenth- and early fifteenth-century Spanish. His chronicles are of great historical value as they are a major source of information concerning events in Spain from 1350 to 1396, and in addition they provide convincing evidence of Ayala as a prose stylist. His long poetic work *Rimado de Palacio* is a highly personal and creative expression of the chancellor's moral and philosophical preoccupations.

Chapter Two

The Chronicles:
Plan, Themes, and Personages

Materials and Manuscripts

The chronicles of Pedro I, Enrique II, Juan I, and Enrique III were written by Pero López de Ayala, probably during the last years of his life. The information contained in the chronicles is based on the author's memory of events as well as on documentary evidence. Since the contents deal mainly with the lives of kings and with events of national importance, other information is omitted that would be of considerable interest to the modern reader. Such matters as social and economic issues or the status of the poor or of women are generally not included. Nevertheless, due to the loss of documentary evidence from Castile of the fourteenth century, much of what we know of the period derives from Ayala's chronicles. As the use of the term *chronicle* implies, the events recorded are usually arranged chronologically. The chronicles are divided into year and chapter segments that impose a certain orderliness upon the material. Often the last chapter of the year contains a brief summary of events in other countries, especially in France. The chronicle of Enrique II contains only one such summary, while approximately half the years in the chronicles of Pedro I and Juan I end this way. Since Castile was not allied with France during the reign of Pedro I, fewer of the summary chapters deal with that country. Some manuscripts of the chronicle of Enrique III end with several chapters detailing events in the papal court at Avignon and a long chapter describing the meeting between the kings of England and France.

The *Chronicle of King Don Pedro* is preceded by a preface that deals primarily with the purpose for writing chronicles. Then follows a table of contents made up of the chapter headings from all four chronicles. The chronicle of Pedro I is the longest, consisting of 164 folios in which are recounted events of the nineteen-year reign. The monarchy of Enrique II, although spanning eleven years of undisputed rule, is chronicled in only thirty-two folios. The chronicles of Juan I and Enrique

III are nearly identical in number of folios, although they respectively cover reigns of twelve and five years.[1] All the manuscripts in existence today are scribal copies of the originals directly written or supervised by the chancellor. More than twenty manuscripts from the fifteenth century survive, indicating a rather wide distribution of the chronicles. Most of the codices contain the chronicles of the first three kings. Early manuscripts containing the chronicle of Enrique III are much rarer and only exist in the so-called *abreviada* version.

The two traditions of the Ayala chronicles were first discussed and subsequently named *abreviada* and *vulgar* by Gerónimo Zurita, royal historian of Aragon in the seventeenth century. The annual nature of the manuscripts in the *vulgar* tradition is emphasized by numbering the chapters within the respective year divisions, while in the *abreviada* the chapters are numbered consecutively from the reign of Pedro I to the end. In general, the *vulgar* version of the chronicles of Pedro I, Enrique II, and Juan I consists of texts that include more extensive sections, as Zurita's denomination suggests. It has been thought that the *abreviada* version was written first; however, Michel Garcia has offered some interesting hypotheses regarding the process of revision of the chronicles. He proposes one stage in which the *abreviada* was written first and later partially revised by Ayala himself and a second when others continued the revisions after Ayala's death. Garcia further theorizes that all the existing codices mix the two versions, the *vulgar* representing a revised first part and an original second part, while the *abreviada* begins with the primitive version and ends with the revised one.[2] In Ayala's revision after the reconciliation of the two dynastic lines, some of the harsher condemnations of Pedro I were removed and the contents were polished, somewhat expanded, and reordered. In these four chronicles, the author relates a series of events more varied and fascinating than many fictional sagas, consisting of wars, fratricides, marriages, mistresses, international intrigues, and power struggles at the highest levels of government.

Pedro I: A Turbulent Beginning

Pedro I, the only surviving son of Alfonso XI and María of Portugal, assumed the throne of Castile and León on 27 March 1350, the day of the death of his father. Unfortunately, Pedro was only sixteen years old and poorly prepared to assume royal responsibility. His upbringing was hampered by lack of contact with his father and a faulty education.

In addition, his mother's hatred for King Alfonso's mistress, Leonor de Guzmán, undoubtedly had an important psychological effect on the young king. Pedro's reign was a turbulent period of history due to constant struggles for power between the king and the nobility, especially the family of Doña Leonor de Guzmán and her illegitimate children by Alfonso XI: Enrique, Fadrique, Fernando, Tello, Juan, Sancho, Pedro, and Juana.

The events of the first year of Pedro's reign are typical of the intrigues and shifting alliances characteristic of the entire period. The first conflict between the king and his opponents, led by Pedro's half-brother Enrique, occurs almost immediately after the coronation because of discontent with official appointments. Doña Leonor de Guzmán, considered a great threat to the monarchy because of her relationship with the former king, was taken prisoner by order of the king. By design of Doña Leonor, the marriage was performed in the prison between her son Enrique and Doña Juana, daughter of Don Juan Manuel and great granddaughter of Fernando de la Cerda, eldest son of King Alfonso X. Ayala reports that "Doña Leonor talked to her son the count about having the wedding with the aforementioned Doña Juana. Therefore the count did it, and secretly consummated the marriage in that palace where Doña Juana was with his mother, Doña Leonor."[3] The principal motive for the marriage of Enrique to Juana was to provide his offspring with legitimate royal ancestry. This event so angered the king and his party that Doña Leonor was taken to Carmona where her incarceration was made even stricter. As the king was about to seize Enrique, the latter disguised himself and succeeded in fleeing to Asturias.

The grave illness that befell the king in August 1350 precipitated a serious crisis in regard to the successor to the throne. Among the main contenders were two principal figures: the Infante Ferrando of Aragon, supported by Juan Alfonso de Alburquerque, the queen mother's counselor, and Juan Núñez de Lara. Both attempted to arrange a marriage with Pedro's mother in order to obtain the support of Doña María's father, the king of Portugal. Because of their illegitimacy, Pedro's half-brothers were not considered possible successors to the throne. However, the timely recovery of the king terminated these intrigues. The death of Juan Núñez a short time later and the seizure of his lands by the king favored Alburquerque, who further strengthened his position by placing wealthy Samuel Levi at the head of the royal treasury. Thus by the end of the first year of Pedro's reign, Juan Alfonso de Alburquerque had assumed total control of the monarchy while the king devoted himself to hunting instead of governing. There is ample evidence of the strong influence that the queen mother and Alburquerque had on the young king. Early in the second year of Pedro's reign, his mother ordered the murder of Doña Leonor de Guzmán, a dangerous action considering the power of her sons and their supporters. Some significant conflicts between the king and the nobles, including Pedro's half-brothers, developed during this time. Although some nobles were punished by death for their rebellious acts, Pedro reacted mildly to the disturbances caused by his half-brothers. He seemingly was more interested in maintaining peace than in seeking punishment or vengeance. Pedro had taken the city of Gijón and seized Enrique's wife. Later, he not only released her but also returned all of the confiscated cities and lands that belonged to Enrique. He only exacted the promise that they would never again rebel against him.

A Political Marriage with Disastrous Results

By the end of the third year of Pedro's reign, the borders of the kingdom appeared secure. Pedro had arranged a truce with the Moors in the south and had obtained the allegiance of the people of Vizcaya. In their meetings with Pedro, the kings of Portugal and Navarre agreed to continue the good relationships that had existed during the reign of Alfonso XI. To further strengthen the realm, the queen mother and Alburquerque favored an alliance with France cemented by the marriage of Pedro and Blanca de Borbón. The marriage, which took place on 3 June 1353, was immediately doomed by Doña Blanca's failure to bring the money promised in her dowry and by Pedro's attachment to his mistress, María de Padilla. After only a few days Pedro left his young queen to return to Doña María. The failure of the marriage destroyed Juan Alfonso's influence with the king. Juan Alfonso so distrusted the king that he fled to Portugal. The king issued orders that anyone who had received an official post with Alburquerque's help was to be removed from his position. Furthermore, Pedro seized all of Alburquerque's lands but made the mistake of appointing his half-brothers Enrique and Fadrique frontier commanders. Alburquerque immediately allied himself with the brothers, his former enemies. The three conspired to support the Infante Pedro of Portugal as king of Castile. The Infante was at first pleased with the plan, but his father soon persuaded him to ignore it.

Although the conspirators seemed thwarted at this point, events occurred in Castile that soon strengthened their position. Ten months after his marriage to Doña Blanca, Pedro decided to marry Juana de Castro, a beautiful widow of noble lineage. When Doña Juana protested that he was already married, Pedro found two bishops who out of fear of the king declared that the marriage to Blanca was null and therefore the king was free to marry whomever he wished. On the day following the marriage, Pedro left Doña Juana and never saw her again. The king's enemies quickly took advantage of this situation and convinced Ferrando de Castro, Juana's brother, to join them in their rebellion.

Another of Pedro's decisions that produced disastrous results was his order that Doña Blanca be taken from Arévalo to the palace in Toledo. When Blanca arrived in Toledo, she took refuge in a church on the pretext of wanting to pray there. Once within the church, she refused to leave because she feared that the king had ordered her death. When Doña Blanca communicated her fears to many important women of the city, they felt great pity for the young queen and determined to help her: "And they talked with their husbands and their relatives, telling them that they would be the most cowardly men in the world if such a queen as that one, who was their mistress, wife of their lord the king, were to die such a death in the city where they were . . ." (57). As a result of the persuasive arguments advanced by the women and also because of growing discontent with the power exercised by the family of María de Padilla, the people of Toledo rose in rebellion against the king. They were quickly joined by several other important cities. Encouraged by the queen mother, the nobles insisted that Pedro have a conference with them in Toro. By this time, the king was virtually without support and had to accede to the demands made on him. Juan Alfonso de Alburquerque had died some months earlier but, according to his request, his vassals had carried his body along with them until the king satisfied the demands made on him. When they saw that the king was going to Toro, the vassals of Juan Alfonso agreed to bury the body of their lord. Once the king was imprisoned in Toro, the nobles forgot the idealistic aspect of their motives and divided the official posts among themselves. Although the king was not allowed to talk with those he wished to during his imprisonment, he was allowed to go hunting each morning. As unity among his opponents disintegrated, many of the nobles took advantage of these hunting periods to approach the king and declare their support for him. Early one very foggy morning the king simply rode away from Toro and thereby escaped from his captors. Only the queen mother, Pedro's half-brothers Enrique, Fadrique, and Tello, and Ferrando de Castro were disturbed by the escape as most of the others had already made their peace with the king.

War with Aragon and the Aftermath of Toro

In spite of the king's apparent forgiveness of the rebels, he spent most of the next two years seeking out and punishing those who had been involved in his imprisonment. The pope's legate Don Guillén tried without success to reconcile Pedro and his family. Enrique succeeded in fleeing to France, and the king's mother was allowed to return to Portugal where she died the following year. Near the end of 1356 war broke out with Aragon because a Catalonian fleet seized two Genoese ships in a Castilian harbor. The king of Aragon ignored Pedro's demands that the ships be released and that the captain responsible for their seizure be turned over to him. At the request of King Pere of Aragon, Enrique and many other Castilian nobles who had taken refuge in France went to Aragon to help in the war against Castile. After several trips between Castile and Aragon, Don Guillén succeeded in arranging a one-year truce. Pedro took advantage of the lull in the fighting to find more of those involved in the uprising at Toro and to have them killed. Pedro seemed especially obsessed with vengeance on his half-brothers and his cousins the Infantes of Aragon. By promising to give Vizcaya to the Infante Juan of Aragon, the king gained his assistance in a plot to kill his half-brother Fadrique. The first fratricide during Pedro's reign took place on 29 May 1358 and is described in great detail in the chronicle.

The same day that Fadrique was killed Pedro set out for Vizcaya to kill another half-brother, Tello. However, Tello was forewarned and fled to Bayonne. Instead of giving Vizcaya to the Infante don Juan as he had promised, Pedro had the Infante killed. When the Infante Ferrando of Aragon, brother of the slain Don Juan, learned of this deed, he broke the truce and entered through the Murcia side of Castile. At the same time, Enrique, angered by the death of Fadrique, invaded through Soria. Don Pedro prepared a fleet to wage war on the sea, but most of the ships were destroyed in a severe storm. The pope again intervened in an effort to restore peace, but the lengthy negotiations failed. Pedro, irritated by the participation of many Castilians in the war against him, vented his anger by ordering the death of his aunt

Doña Leonor, mother of the Infante Ferrando; Doña Juana de Lara, wife of Don Tello; Doña Isabel, sister of Doña Juana; and his two half-brothers Juan and Pedro. The war continued until 1361 when Pedro learned that the king of Granada was considering entering the war on the side of the king of Aragon. Since Pedro could not risk war simultaneously on two frontiers, he begrudgingly made peace with Aragon.

In spite of sporadic truces arranged by the pope's legate, the war with Aragon continued throughout the remainder of Pedro's reign. Early in 1363 Pedro arranged an important alliance with the king of England and his son the Prince of Wales. During these years the number of Enrique's supporters increased greatly. With financial aid from the kings of France and Aragon, he obtained the services of some bands of soldiers with whom he had fought in France. The leader of these companies was the French knight Bertrand Du Guesclin. With this help Enrique invaded Castile early in 1366 and easily took possession of Calahorra. Enrique's supporters tried to convince him to proclaim himself king of Castile. Enrique did not agree at once; however, he seemed pleased by the suggestion and soon allowed himself to be convinced by his followers. Don Pedro was in Burgos at the time, but when he learned that Enrique and his army were coming, he left the city, accompanied by only a few supporters. The majority of the other nobles either joined Enrique or left Burgos to return to their own lands. Enrique successively took Burgos (where he was crowned), Toledo, and Seville. Pedro was forced to flee to Galicia and from there to Bayonne in order to seek aid from his English allies.

The king of Navarre promised Enrique that he would not allow Pedro, the Prince of Wales, and their forces to pass through his lands. Furthermore, he assured Enrique of his help if a battle did occur. When Pedro and his allies arrived, the king of Navarre not only permitted them passage but also vowed to participate in the battle on their side. To avoid being involved in the battle at all, he then arranged with a noble to be taken prisoner and held in the castle of Borja for the duration of the war. The campaign was at first favorable to Enrique, but because of the strong support of the Prince of Wales and the flight of Enrique's brother Tello during the fighting, Pedro was victorious in the Battle of Nájera in 1367. Enrique was again obliged to flee to France. A short time later Pedro was deserted by the English prince, who was disturbed by Pedro's cruel treatment of the prisoners and dissatisfied with the king's failure to supply wages and lands promised to him and his men before the war.

During the five months of Enrique's stay in France, he was able to arrange an alliance with King Charles V. Upon returning to Castilian territory, Enrique dismounted, knelt on the ground, drew a cross in the sand, kissed it, and said: "I swear by this sign of the cross that never in my life will I leave the kingdom of Castile, no matter how necessary it may be, and here I will await the death or good fortune that may come to me" (181). As Enrique took city after city, Don Pedro sought aid from the Moors of Granada. During their attack on Córdoba, the Moors succeeded in gaining entrance to the city, whereupon the women of the city went out into the streets, their hair flowing about them, to plead with the men of Córdoba to save them from captivity by the Moors. The men were so inspired and moved by the women's tears and words that they were able to expel the Moors from the city. On their way back to Granada, the Moors sacked and burned Jaén and Ubeda.

As the situation became more critical, Pedro fortified Carmona and took his children and treasure there. He then left to try to help the besieged people of Toledo. When Enrique discovered Pedro's plans, he and his army set out on an all-night march to trap Pedro at Montiel. The following day Pedro's sparse forces were defeated. Along with a few followers, he took refuge in the castle of Montiel. To prevent Pedro's escape, Enrique built a wall around the castle and heavily guarded it day and night. Ironically, Pedro's last attempt to save himself resulted in his capture. Through one of his men Pedro tried to convince Bertrand Du Guesclin to help him escape. Bertrand refused to do what he felt would be a dishonorable act. He reported his conversation to Enrique, who suggested that Du Guesclin pretend to help Pedro in order to get him to leave the castle. When Pedro arrived at Bertrand's lodgings, he was seized and held there until Enrique arrived. Enrique then attacked and stabbed his half-brother to death. Thus the civil war and the reign of Pedro I ended on 23 March 1369.

Enrique II: The First Three Years

The death of Pedro I removed Enrique's immediate rival for the throne, but a number of problems still confronted him, the two most pressing being the weakness of the frontiers, because of rebellion of border towns and threats of invasion by the kings of Granada and

Portugal, and the lack of resources to pay foreign and domestic troops. The efforts of the first Trastamaran monarch during the initial three years of his reign were directed toward the solution of these difficulties. The new money minted to alleviate the economic strain only served to aggravate the situation and increase inflation. To ensure the support of the nobles and to pay the French troops, Enrique relinquished many of the lands belonging to the crown, thereby further reducing income of the royal treasury. In the Cortes of 1371, the nobles succeeded in persuading the king not to reapportion the *behetrías*. Moreover, the currency was devalued and no more could be minted until the king had more wealth in the treasury. The treasure won in a naval battle against the English at the end of this year provided some economic relief and enabled Enrique to buy back some cities from his French ally Bertrand Du Guesclin.

Because of the frontier difficulties, the new king found it necessary to travel from one problem area to another during the remaining months of 1369 trying to establish control over the kingdom. Almost immediately after Pedro's death, Enrique journeyed to Seville to procure the allegiance of the Andalusian towns, to provide a defense against the Moorish king who refused to renew the treaty, and to try to take Carmona where the former king's children and treasury were being guarded. In the meanwhile La Coruña and all of Galicia, plus Zamora and other western cities, had declared in favor of Fernando I of Portugal. After appointing frontier governors in the south and sending his wife and son Juan to await him in the imperial city of Toledo, the king hastened to Galicia where he and his army invaded Portugal "to make friends" with the neighboring monarch. Three of the most powerful nobles still loyal to Pedro I and his heirs led the resistance against Enrique: Ferrando de Castro in Galicia, and Martín López de Córdoba and Matheos Ferrández de Cáceres in Carmona.

During 1370 the same problems continued; however, the situation was improved by a truce with the king of Granada and by the death of Enrique's brother Tello which, with the acceptance of the Infante don Juan as Lord of Vizcaya, gave the crown direct control over that region. Although there was no proof, it was rumored that the king ordered his physician to poison Tello because the latter frequently had dealings with those who opposed Enrique. Early in 1371 Carmona was finally taken by means of an agreement with Martín López who, in exchange for an assurance of his own safety, agreed to betray his companion and hand the city over to Enrique. Although Martín López is described as a self-interested traitor, Enrique himself did not escape criticism by his loyalists when he ordered the death of both Martín López and Matheos Ferrández. After a long seige Zamora also was finally regained, and Ferrando de Castro was defeated in Galicia and driven back to Portugal. By the end of the third year of Enrique's reign, most of the rebellious areas had been subdued and truces had been arranged with the neighboring kingdoms.

Matrimonial Politics

Narration of events in 1372 and 1373 is devoted mainly to the renewed antagonism between Spain and Portugal. The insurance for the 1371 peace treaty was to have been a marriage between Ferrando I of Portugal and Enrique's daughter Leonor. This agreement was doomed by Ferrando's declaration that he could not marry the Infanta because he was already married to Leonor Téllez. The failure of the Portuguese king to honor his word was only one of the justifications presented by the chronicler for Enrique to invade Portugal. Ferrando violated the treaty by seizing some Spanish ships, which he later refused to give up because of his enmity toward the Spanish king. Rebel knights on both sides provided further reasons for the invasion: the Castilians using Portugal to make forays into Galicia and many Portuguese, including Ferrando's brother, indicating their desire to join Enrique. In spite of the arrival in Spain of the papal legate who hoped to serve as mediator between the two kings, Enrique decided to invade Portugal "to make the King don Ferrando be his friend or to destroy his land" (BAE, 15). Enrique successfully penetrated into Portugal where his troops burned parts of Lisbon, and his fleet recaptured the Castilian ships. From this position of strength the Castilian monarch agreed to cooperate with the papal representative in his efforts to arrange peace terms. Enrique remained in Portugal until the rebellious Castilian knights, including Ferrando de Castro, were expelled from the country and one of the three proposed marriages was carried out between members of the two royal families.

Throughout his reign Enrique II attempted to use marriages as his principal diplomatic tactic in securing his borders and increasing Castilian control over neighboring kingdoms, although, as was the case in Portugal, he did not hesitate to use military force also. In addition to the Portuguese marital alliances, a double wedding took place in 1375 in which the Infante Juan, the Trastamaran heir, married Leonor of Aragon, and Leonor of Castile wed Carlos, the future king of Navarre. The exiled supporters of the heirs of Pedro I encouraged the marriage of the duke of Lancaster to Costanza, daughter and heir of Pedro I, and the subsequent claim by the duke to be the rightful king of Castile. The alliances of Lancaster with Aragon and especially with Portugal continued to be a threat to the Trastamaran dynasty for more than a decade and a half until another wedding in 1388, between the duke's daughter and the future Enrique III, finally united the two royal pretenders to the throne.

The Spanish Armada and the French Connection

The first time that Enrique II sent his fleet into battle, in 1370, was an almost comical disaster. Pedro I had ordered all the oars in Seville taken to Carmona and locked up there so that Enrique would not be able to make use of the ships. Enrique, however, refused to heed the objections of his sailors and insisted that they sail out to fight the Portuguese fleet which was menacing Seville. No battle took place because, without the oars, the Castilian ships could not follow the Portuguese to the high seas. In 1371 a significant sea victory against the English helped alleviate Enrique's financial problems, and by 1372 he was able to begin to fulfill his annual commitment to send ships to help France against the English in the Hundred Years' War. The power and success of the Spanish fleet increased so much in the next few years that, early in the reign of Juan I, the Spanish ships even sailed up the Thames River.

The Spanish-English sea battles were a direct result of the Trastamaran alliance with France that began with the French mercenaries who helped Enrique invade Castile, overthrow his brother, who was allied with the English, and subdue the neighboring peninsular kingdoms. Throughout his reign, the French alliance was the dominant factor in Castilian foreign affairs. The war with Navarre (1378–79) was instigated by the French who accused the Navarrese king of plotting to join the English against France and Castile. When Enrique sent his army to enter Navarre, Ayala commented: "And the King don Enrique did this to fulfill the obligations and agreements that he had with the King of France" (BAE, 33). One incident near the end of Enrique's reign when he resisted French influence was his decision to remain neutral in the dispute between the two claimants to the papal throne. Surprisingly, the monarchs of the Iberian Peninsula at first were united in their determination to maintain neutrality, even though eventually they tended to join the side favored by their allies—England or France.

What Manner of King Is This?

The religious aspect of Enrique's nature receives emphasis only near the end of his life, as is evident in his concern about the schism in the church and in his desire to receive the sacraments during his last illness. In the final description of the king after his death, Ayala observes that Enrique was intelligent, forceful, frank, fortunate, and good at dealing with and honoring people. The chronicler does not specify any negative characteristics although some less praiseworthy aspects are readily observable. An attribute that the chronicler does not name but which is apparent in Enrique's words and actions is his impatience and irascibility. These qualities are evident throughout the chronicle, for example, in the seige of Carmona while his men are trapped inside the city; when Fernando of Portugal seizes his ships; when the king of Navarre plots to join the English and betray France; and finally on his deathbed. In the latter episode the king awoke at dawn and demanded that mass be said, but as his confessor did not come rapidly enough, Enrique began to complain, and he himself appealed directly to God. He never liked to act through intermediaries, preferring to be in direct control of situations, always showing himself to be decisive, dynamic, and forceful.

He placed a high value on loyalty, as is evident in his respectful fulfillment of his father's will (Alfonso XI), in his relations with France, and in the episode of the knight who was offended by the king of Aragon (1376; chap. 2). Nevertheless, the Trastamaran king was not averse to using deception to serve his purposes, for example, when he ignored his promise to Martín López at Carmona and ordered him killed, or when he tried to trick the king of Navarre into entering Logroño (1378). It is possible that Enrique was involved in the death of his brother Tello, and he was criticized for ordering the death of the two knights at Carmona. Early in Enrique's reign, the knight who had been guarding Ferrando de Castro when the latter escaped feared the king so much that he chose to follow Ferrando de Castro rather than remain in Castile. Even though he faced certain imprisonment and possible death, it was preferable to facing the wrath of Enrique. In another instance in 1371, however, the deaths ordered by the king in retribution for the killing of his brother-in-law Felipe de Castro

are viewed as an act of justice. When his brother Sancho was killed
in a fight by a man who did not recognize him, the king's reaction is
described this way: "And it grieved the king very much, and he wanted
to inflict great punishment; but he found out afterwards that it happened
by chance, and they advised him not to kill anyone because of it,
except some men of little worth who were involved in the fight" (BAE,
22). Reason and restraint are also evident in the king's dealings with
the Cortes and with his council. In fact, when the countess of Alanzón
claims the lands of Lara and Vizcaya, Enrique is shown as a shrewd
diplomat who is able to avoid giving up the lands. In addition to the
many references to his justice and loyalty, Enrique himself specifically
comments on the king's duties in a message to the king of Aragon
saying: "for you, Sir, are King and judge, and you should be the same
to all parties" (BAE, 30). Also subject to frequent mention in the
chronicle are Enrique's royal lineage, particularly through his marriage
to Juana Manuel, his great power, and the love the people have for
him. The positive qualities, which are mentioned or seen with increasing
frequency starting in 1371, are evidence of Ayala's concept of the
monarchy but also of the importance he places on the justification of
Enrique as the rightful ruler of the kingdom.

The King Is Dead, Long Live the King!: The Importance of Continuity

In the midst of the festivities celebrating the crowning of Juan I,
the second Trastamaran monarch, a delegation of distinguished gentlemen
from the *aljama,* or Jewish quarter, approached the young king with
a request based on time-honored tradition. As Juan was eager to maintain
ancient customs, a trait that persists throughout his reign, he granted
them a royal decree stating that their governor had the right to have
a Jewish troublemaker killed. When Juan later learned that the troublemaker was actually Iusaf Pichón, a Jewish court official during his
father's reign, he was so amazed and angry that such a deception took
place, especially during his coronation, that he had the group of Jews
seized and killed. The official who was involved was also arrested but,
since he had been deceived into believing that he was carrying out the
king's orders, he was not killed but only had his hand cut off. The
dramatic re-creation of this event, which forms the core of the narration
of the first year of Juan I's reign, is more than a device to attract the

reader's attention, although undoubtedly it functions admirably in this respect. The episode has a strong anti-Semitic tone, portraying Spanish Jews as devious, untrustworthy, and incapable of judicious self-government. Juan's decision to take away the right of the Jews to punish evildoers in their midst resulted in the suppression of the autonomy of the Jewish communities and is evidence of the continually increasing hostility toward Spanish Jewry that led finally to the pogroms of 1391. Juan's action exonerates him from any blame in the matter while simultaneously portraying him as a just king who deals firmly with problems.

The establishment of Juan's character and his approach to the monarchy are part of the vitally important ongoing process of justification of the Trastámara line. Although Juan's father, Enrique II, had succeeded in bringing together most of the various regions and factions in the kingdom, the importance of continuity is evident from the beginning in the oath that Juan makes on the day of his coronation, 21 June 1379, in Burgos, the same city where his father had been crowned some fourteen years earlier. His vow "to guard the freedoms and liberties and good uses and good customs of the kingdom" (65) serves as the early basis of his reign. Since he is to continue the work begun by his father, it is important to affirm the concept of Enrique II as the rightful monarch of Castile and León. The birth of a son to Juan and his wife Leonor provides an opportunity to exalt the memory of the former king. Referring to the birth of the heir to the throne, Ayala writes: "And the kingdom took great pleasure in his birth, especially because he had the name of his grandfather, the King Don Enrique, who had been very loved by all, for he had brought great honor to the kingdom and had been feared by all its neighbors" (67). Juan's travels through the realm, accompanied by the body of his father, during the last half of 1379 and the eventual arrival in Toledo early in 1380 serve a dual purpose. The journey and state funeral, carried out with great ceremony, continue to honor Enrique's memory while affording an opportunity for the people to become better acquainted with the new king.

Others who must test the mettle of Juan I are Spain's immediate neighbors, France and Portugal. Relations with these two countries continue to be the most important factors in foreign affairs during his reign. Because of a truce with the king of Granada, the Reconquest is not a problem at this time. The alliance with France was first formed by the then Count Enrique to aid in his struggle against his half-brother Pedro I and thereafter is faithfully maintained by Juan I throughout his reign. The importance attached to this alliance is evidenced by the fact that in the narration of the first year of Juan's reign, two of the five chapters are dedicated to relations with the French, while in the second year four of the nine chapters deal with this topic. In addition to the messengers from France who arrive at Juan's court, the king of the other neighboring country, Portugal, also sends his messengers. Fernando of Portugal has a suggestion that greatly interests Juan: that they set aside the marriage that had been arranged during the previous reign between Fernando's only child, Beatriz, and Fadrique, son of Enrique II. He proposes instead that she marry the Infante Enrique, the newborn son of Juan I. Furthermore, if either of the two kings dies without a legitimate heir, the other will be his successor. This plan forms an early basis for Juan's desire to unite the two kingdoms, a factor that nearly ruined Castile and led to one of the most serious Castilian defeats: Aljubarrota.

The Character of the Monarch

Several other incidents happen in 1380 which in themselves are not of great import, but which are used by the chronicler to reveal aspects of Juan's character and to give examples of how the monarchy functions. The idea of the king as the careful dispenser of justice recurs when a plot is discovered between Juan's brother Alfonso and Pero Manrique, one of the highest government officials in Castile. Not only is the case investigated openly, but Manrique's family is consulted before any punishment is carried out. Juan is shown to be a generous and wise peacemaker when, after the death of Charles V of France, he helps to mediate a dispute between the duke of Anjou and the king of Aragon. His swift response to the pleas for help from the imprisoned king of Armenia reveal his pious, empathetic nature. Mention of his stance as a warrior against the enemies of the faith leads naturally to consideration of two religious problems, one national and the other international. A symptom of the internal problem between the clergy and the nobility that continues to surface in many of the Cortes is seen in the complaint of the monasteries that some noblemen are taking rents and tributes due to the religious orders. In most disputes of this sort, Juan's decisions usually favored the clergy over the nobility. In fact, at one point all but two of the members of his advisory council were clergymen. The other, more serious, dilemma is the choice that had to be made between the two claimants to the papal throne. The decision in favor of the

Avignon pope, Clement VII, is at least partially due to strong French influence. In both of these situations, Juan's method of arriving at a decision after consideration of the advice of a group of the best-qualified advisors becomes typical of his manner of government. Throughout his reign, he rarely makes a decision without consultation with his advisory council. As a member of the council, Ayala is able to give detailed reports of these deliberations, providing numerous examples of the interaction between king and council.

War With Portugal

By 1381, the third year of Juan's reign, it becomes increasingly apparent that peace with Portugal cannot be achieved by arranging marriages between the two royal families. With the help of the English, the Portuguese prepare for war with Castile. Early the next year the situation has deteriorated to the point that two massive armies are gathered, and battle lines are drawn up at Badajoz. A last minute peace is arranged through another switch in the marriage plans. This time, the ten-year-old Portuguese princess Beatriz is to marry Juan's second son, Ferrando, ostensibly to avoid mixing the two kingdoms. A short time later, the death of Juan's wife Leonor in childbirth gives Ferrando of Portugal the idea that Juan himself can marry Beatriz. It is somewhat ironic that, in the same place where they nearly went to war a short time ago, Juan I and all the grandees from both nations swear a solemn oath "on the body of God" (80) that they will abide by the terms of the marriage agreement. After completing their vows, all participate in lavish wedding festivities.

The peaceful interlude is quickly ended by the death of the Portuguese king five months later. There is much uncertainty on both sides of the border about the proper course of action, and there are many who either openly or covertly consider the treaty invalid. Against the advice of some members of his council, Juan decides to break the treaty and enter Portugal with his army. It soon becomes apparent that the real leader of the opposition to Juan is the master of Avis, illegitimate half-brother of the dead King Fernando. To partisans of Juan I, the contrast between the two men must have been disheartening. The Portuguese knights who come to pay homage to Juan are unhappy with the way they are received and with the king's failure to give them gifts. A more serious problem, however, is their negative reaction to his personality. Ayala reports: "Besides, they were not pleased with the king because he was a man of few words, and they were used to King Don Ferrando of Portugal who was a man of great expressiveness" (45). The master of Avis, in contrast, is a man of such power and charisma and so beloved by the people of Lisbon that they riot in the streets after hearing a rumor that he has been killed. They are only prevented from burning the palace by his appearance at the window—assuring them that he is alive and well. Under the dynamic leadership of the master of Avis, the Portuguese continue the war against Castile for another year and a half until the stunning Castilian defeat at Aljubarrota.

Consequences of Defeat at Aljubarrota

The battle of Aljubarrota has a number of grave consequences. The master of Avis, now João I of Portugal, is in firm possession of the Portuguese throne, and the last threat of Portugal being absorbed by Castile is ended. His alliance with England is strengthened by his marriage to Felipa, daughter of the duke of Lancaster. With the encouragement of João of Portugal, the duke and his wife Costanza, daughter of Pedro I, arrive at La Coruña with a sizeable army to reassert their claim to the Castilian crown. Seventeen years after the end of the civil war that put the first Trastamaran monarch on the throne, the entry of the duke and duchess into Galicia poses a serious challenge to the dynasty. The Castilian forces are so decimated that even with the help of French mercenaries they are forced into a purely defensive position on their own soil. The English and Portuguese forces are much stronger than the Castilian remnants but, fortunately for Juan, the English arrive too late in the year to begin a full-scale assault before spring. During the winter, the English army is greatly diminished in size and power due primarily to the plagues. In the meantime, while strategically locating his sparse troops, Juan begins negotiations with the duke designed to end the present threat. His more important motive, however, is to arrange a marriage between their two heirs, who would then inherit Castile and Leon. Although a secret accord is reached, Lancaster cannot resist joining João of Portugal in an unsuccessful invasion attempt in March of 1387. The specific terms of the agreement, which is finally reached in 1388, and the line of inheritance of the throne are discussed in great detail. Many folios of the chronicle are devoted to this pact because of the crucial importance of the definitive settlement of the dynastic quarrel between the heirs of Pedro I and those of Enrique II.

For the Love of Power: The Plan to Renounce the Throne

In order to gain time to rebuild his army and to strengthen his financial position, Juan signs a six-year truce with Portugal. During the Cortes of 1390, however, it is very clear that he has not given up his dream of controlling the neighboring kingdom. With an amazing lack of awareness of the realities of the actual situation, Juan proposes to his council that he renounce the crown of Castile and Leon, divide the kingdom with his young son, and again declare himself king of Portugal. The council unanimously rejects the plan and, in a masterful oration, they convince the king that it would be against his interests to follow such a course of action. Juan's plan to replenish the royal treasury during the truce so that he can invade Portugal again conflicts with his promise to give the cities relief from taxes. The problem of big government, inflated budgets, and excessive military spending has a modern ring. Juan recognizes the validity of the criticism but insists that the crown is not to blame: "It is true that I know that what you say is so, but at times I have started to order it [reform], and all of you, each one of you, ask me to give special consideration to your own area, with the result that there is never any end to it" (132). The problem is resolved by certain military reforms and provision for a regular, standing army.

Among other matters dealt with in this meeting of the Cortes is the rivalry of the church with nobles and cities over jurisdiction, clarification of the procedure for rights of appeal, inheritance of lands given to nobles by Enrique II, and the request by the king of Navarre that his wife return to live with him instead of living at the Castilian court. Soon after the Cortes ended, Juan and some members of his court went to see the *caballeros farfanes*. This is a group of Christian knights who were descendants of the Visigoths and had lived for centuries in Morocco. They had just returned to Castile where the king promised them an inheritance. On 9 October 1390, on his way to visit these knights, Juan I was unexpectedly killed in a fall from his horse.

The Minority of Enrique III

The chronicle of the reign of Enrique III comprises the narration of events during the first five years of this monarch's reign, from the last

months of 1390 until the end of 1395. Fully one third of the work
deals with the grave problem of how the country was to be governed
during the king's minority. The unexpected death of Juan I left an
eleven-year-old boy as ruler of Castile. Most of the nobles of the
kingdom, as well as the representatives of the cities, gathered in Madrid
to acknowledge him as their king and to decide how the kingdom was
to be ruled. The seemingly obvious solution of following the will of
the dead monarch was initially rejected by all present. Juan I had drawn
up the will in 1385 before the Battle of Aljubarrota, and many claimed
that later the king frequently said in his council that he no longer
favored the plan of government established in his will. The archbishop
of Toledo, Pedro Tenorio, suggested rule by one, three, or five persons
as set forth in the second *Partida*. Others proposed a council made up
of representatives from all sectors, reasoning that Juan I had favored
this idea, and furthermore a council had been used in France after the
death of Charles V. The will was treated as a subject for ridicule; in
fact, the archbishop at first claimed ignorance of its existence. He only
remembered it after Ayala, one of the witnesses to the will, reminded
him that the king had sent the will to the archbishop for safekeeping.
The will, eventually found in a chest in the king's chambers, was
considered so worthless that some suggested burning it in the fireplace.
The archbishop of Toledo decided to take the will, saying that even
though the rest of it was invalid, the portions dealing with alms for
the church in Toledo should be honored. All finally agreed to rule by
means of a council; however, some remained discontent, believing that
they would have had more power under a different system. The
government by council seemed doomed from the outset by the archbishop's refusal to support it.

Tragic Consequences: The Pogroms

A tragic consequence of the lack of a recognized ruling authority is
the uprising against the Jews in Seville early in 1391. Against the
background of the anti-Semitic sermons preached by the Archdeacon
Ferrando Martínez, the immediate spark that incited the Sevillans was
the punishment of a Christian for his actions against Jews. All the
people were so stirred up that they took the city judge prisoner and
tried to kill both him and the count of Niebla. The chronicler reports
that letters from the king and the council did little to calm the situation,
for the people "were so aroused, and they feared no one, and their

greedy desire to rob the Jews increased each day" (BAE, 167). The Jewish quarters of many cities were destroyed, including those in Seville, Córdoba, Burgos, Toledo, Logroño, Barcelona, and Valencia. A large part of the Jewish population was killed, and those that survived became very poor because they had to pay large sums for protection. A few months later, news again reached the court that "the city of Seville had robbed the Jewish quarter, and that most of the Jews that were there turned Christian and many of them died" (BAE, 177). Although the king sent letters and soldiers to guard the Jewish communities in other locations, this did not prevent the movement from spreading. The people wanted to attack the Moors also, but they did not dare to do so for fear of reprisals against Christian captives in Granada and overseas. According to Ayala, the people, motivated more by greed than by devotion to the faith, took advantage of the youth of the king and the discord among the nobles in order to rob the Jews.

Where There's a Will . . .

Unrest and division were also growing among the members of the council, to the extent that some brought armed knights with them to meetings. Opposition by the archbishop of Toledo soon resulted in his leaving Madrid and returning to his own lands where he sent out letters to everyone of importance, including the pope, cardinals, rulers of France and Aragon, and many cities in Castile. The letters contained the surprising opinion that the council was invalid because it was contrary to the will left by Juan I. Greed and self-interest led to such mutual distrust and fear that by mid-year the most powerful nobles in the country were divided into two groups, led, respectively, by the archbishop of Toledo and the archbishop of Santiago, Juan García Manrique. The repeated emissaries who tried to convince the archbishop of Toledo to come to a meeting of the Cortes to decide the best way of governing had no success at all. The archbishop, although not rejecting the idea of a solution determined by the Cortes, consistently replied that he favored the will of Juan I and that the council should be dissolved. He further insisted that he could not do anything without consulting those who agreed with his view.

The threat of civil war increased, with the build-up of forces on each side, and the complete lack of order in the country resulted in widespread waste, disruptions, seizures, and robberies. Finally, a delegation of citizens from Burgos proposed to the king that the Cortes be held in their city with their own children serving as hostages. Leonor of Navarre, the young king's aunt, rushed frantically back and forth between the two armed camps, and was finally successful in reconciling opposing members of her family and avoiding the imminent conflict. Extended meetings between representatives of the two sides yielded a compromise that could have been tolerated by all: the former king's will would be followed in the naming of the tutors and representatives of the cities. However, to satisfy the demands of the high nobility, three more tutors would be added, all members of the king's family. When the freeing from prison of Count Alfonso again upset the power balance, Leonor of Navarre succeeded in convincing her relatives that although Alfonso belonged to the opposing group, he was a member of the family and it was possible that he would later join them. The new atmosphere of conciliation was destroyed by the death of a knight allied with Count Alfonso and the implication that the duke of Benavente was involved in the killing. Opposition to the king's family was so great that the city representatives voted unanimously to accept the will of Juan I without any changes or additions. From that day on, it was assumed that the will would be followed.

After such a prolonged dispute, it seems appropriate that Ayala chose to include the will "without adding or taking away a word" (BAE, 185). The extensive testament, which comprises one tenth of the chronicle, contains detailed orders for ruling the kingdom and a list of the persons who should serve as officials, in addition to many other provisions. Among the more picturesque aspects of the will are descriptions of the gold and silk vestments to be made for the church in Toledo, and certain instructions dealing with the funeral ceremonies, for example, on the day of the burial all members of religious orders (monks, nuns, priests, etc.) of the city of Toledo were to attend; six hundred poor were to be clothed, according to specifications given; and they were to be fed for the nine days that the funeral lasted. In addition, one hundred Christian captives—men, women, and children—were to be ransomed from the Moors. Peaceful acceptance of the will seemed unlikely from the start, for Juan had issued many orders during the last year of his life that countermanded various terms of the will. Furthermore, the power struggle between the two groups at court continued, especially concerning money. The chancellor observes that "the tutors never were in accord among themselves, and each one wanted to help the one he liked, and therefore the common good and welfare were often forgotten" (BAE, 196).

The most serious problem facing the nation in the ensuing months was the possibility of war with Portugal. The Portuguese were not eager to sign a truce and were making great demands because the duke of Benavente had agreed to marry the illegitimate daughter of the king of Portugal, thus giving the latter a powerful ally in western Castile. The focus of attention in this portion of the chronicle alternates between two negotiating efforts. While the Castilian and Portuguese truce negotiators prolonged their deliberations, each side waited for a final decision from the duke. The archbishop of Toledo shuttled back and forth between the king's court and the duke's palace, trying to convince the latter that the proposed marriage was neither in his honor nor in the king's service. The situation was especially grave due to the king's youth, the unrest in the kingdom, and the lack of money for a war. In spite of the archbishop's efforts, the duke continued to insist that he could not serve the king as he would like to because he had been shut out of the government and had not received the money due to him. He also added that he did not trust those who were with the king and had to protect himself against persons who would harm him. The threat of war with Portugal was avoided by the decision to accept the unfavorable terms of the treaty, but once again civil war loomed unavoidably as the duke built up his army and decided to take over the city of Zamora. The duke's army was lost in the fog all night and when they finally reached Zamora, it was already under the control of the king's troops. The archbishop of Toledo's inability to change the duke's course of action, and the latter's subsequent unsuccessful military action resulted in a shift of power in the king's court. For the next one half year, the archbishop of Santiago and the lesser nobility dominated the government of Castile.

The King Takes Over

According to the terms of Juan I's will, the tutors were to rule until Enrique reached the age of fourteen. In August 1393, two months before his fourteenth birthday, the young king declared that he wanted to take over the kingdom, and that the tutors would no longer rule because "they themselves said it was not done as it should be" (BAE, 211). The king and his council called for the Cortes to be convened after Enrique's birthday. In the interval, the monarch traveled north to receive the Seigniory of Vizcaya, fulfilling the local law which required the feudal lord to personally take possession of the territory. At the

Cortes, all offices and favors given out by the tutors were revoked, and bookkeepers were appointed to draw up lists of all lands and favors. Ayala points out that because the king was so young, his advisors had him order other expenses, saying it was in his interest, and "what they did not dare do before the age of fourteen, they did after fourteen" (BAE, 216). With the end of the Cortes, which were of short duration because of illness in Madrid, early in 1394 the king went to Illescas to see the archbishop of Toledo. This, of course, angered the latter's old rival the archbishop of Santiago who, claiming illness, left the court and went to meet with the duke of Benavente. The king's relatives, upset by reduced revenues, were again joining forces, and the duke was defiantly collecting monies that should have been paid to the king's treasurers.

At this inopportune moment, messengers arrived with news that the master of Alcantara, with a small army, had decided to invade and conquer Granada. In spite of the truce with the Moorish kingdom and the impossibility of success, the master of Alcantara was determined not to turn back because it would be a great dishonor, and, moreover, a hermit who accompanied him had seen a vision of a miraculous victory over the infidels. In the ensuing battle the master, all of his lancers, and many of the foot soldiers were killed. Because of uncertainty over whether the truce would be kept, the council made the mistake of sending letters to all the king's vassals, including the duke of Benavente and counts Alfonso and Pedro, requesting that they gather their troops and come to help the king. The truce with Granada was quickly reaffirmed, but armed conflict between the king's forces and those of his relatives appeared likely. In this dangerous situation, some of the king's advisors favored confrontation, while others advocated conciliation. The king's family seemed unable to unite in any forceful action and, one by one, were definitively eliminated as threats to the monarchy. In quick succession, the duke of Benavente was arrested and imprisoned in Burgos; the queen of Navarre was returned under guard to her husband; Count Alfonso's last stronghold in Gijon was destroyed, and he was permanently exiled; and Count Pedro was pardoned but not allowed to return to the court. The last mention of Enrique III in this chronicle finds the young monarch securely established in his palace in Seville after a joyous reception by the people of Andalusia.[4]

Chapter Three

The Chronicler's Motives and Narrative Technique

The Chronicler's Motives

The epoch that Ayala chronicles, from the ascension to the throne of Pedro I in 1350 until the fifth year of the reign of Enrique III in 1395, was a period of crisis and of such peninsular and international conflicts as civil and religious wars in Spain, the Hundred Years' War and the schism of the church. Upon describing this era, Lapesa recalls "a Castile bloodied by monarchical individualism, insane cruelties and fratricidal wars. . . ."[1] The dominant motives of the chronicler who witnessed this epoch may spring from his personal ambition and his national consciousness, but he is also inspired by his religious faith and his preoccupation with the moral significance of historical events. Just as Alfonso el Sabio (the Learned) had done a century earlier, Ayala prominently expresses his intention in his prologue. He wants to chronicle events and deeds so that one can learn to direct well the matters of state as well as one's own personal conduct. He considers events as the fulfillment of divine will with history serving to teach truths about the conduct of kings, nobles, and statesmen. In his prologue, Ayala identifies himself with the purpose and norms of ancient chroniclers:

And from then on it was the custom for princes and kings to order books to be prepared, which were called chronicles and histories, in which chivalresque deeds, and many other things that ancient princes did, were recorded so that those that came after them might make a better and greater effort to do good and to guard against doing evil. . . . Therefore, henceforth I, Pero López de Ayala, with the help of God, intend to continue thus, and as truly as I am able, concerning what I saw, in which I intend nothing more than to tell the truth. Moreover, in regard to what happened in my age and time in other areas where I was not present, I know about it from the true report of gentlemen and knights and other trustworthy persons from whom I heard it. And they gave me their testimony, taking it with the greatest diligence I could. (1)

Throughout the chronicle of Pedro I, one notices the moral-didactic purpose, about which Robert B. Tate observes: "The *Chronicle* besides being a thesis is, like the *Rimado,* a manual of political education, a lesson in the way to observe and judge daily actions of our neighbors."[2] The posture of Ayala as a moralist is firmly established in a passage at the beginning of the second year of the reign of Pedro I. In these lines he records the reaction of many people after the assassination of Doña Leonor de Guzmán: "And this grieved many in the kingdom a great deal, for they understood that from a deed such as this would come great wars and disturbances in the kingdom, as happened later, because Doña Leonor had grown sons and many relatives. And in events like this, for the sake of a little vengeance many evils and dangers are later created, and it would be much better to avoid them: for much evil and much war was born in Castile for this reason" (22).

In general, Ayala's narration of the deaths ordered by Pedro I is accompanied by either the reactions of persons who lament and criticize the violence of the king or by the chronicler's own comments about the innocence of the victims and how unjust these acts seem. In short, this is the posture of a person who judges others on moral grounds. Thus what happened to the two princes, Don Pedro and Don Juan, "greatly grieved those who were devoted to the king's service because they died this way, for they were innocent, and they had never wronged the king" (109). Sometimes the chronicler communicates his moralizing point of view directly, without making use of the criticisms or reactions of others. He does this by means of such observations as "and thus came the judgments of God" (50) or "therefore much evil came to Castile" (122). There are numerous occasions in the chronicle of Pedro I when the king's actions are used as a negative example. One of the few instances when Pedro shows mercy takes place after he put down the uprising of the people of Toledo. An eighty-year-old silversmith was condemned to die for his participation. The old man's son, who was only eighteen, approached the king and pleaded that he be allowed to give his life in exchange for his father's freedom. The chronicler notes that everyone was pleased when Pedro ordered that neither the man nor his son be killed. Although the action impresses by virtue of its rarity, its effect is nearly lost, as Ayala sandwiches it in between reports of the imprisonment and death of many good knights of the city.

In the chronicle of Enrique II, there is really no moralizing of the sort that is so prevalent in the chronicle of Pedro I. In the case of the death of Enrique's brother Tello, although Ayala reports the implication of guilt on the king's part, he makes no moral judgment. He simply comments that "this is not a certainty, but rather a rumor that it was this way" (BAE, 8). In another instance, after taking the city of Carmona, Enrique II ordered Martín López to be killed. Many who were devoted to the king's service complained and tried to prevent his death. The master of Santiago, Ferrand Osores, had pledged to Martín López that the king would assure his safety. Although he had done this under orders from the king, Osores felt that López's death represented a failure to keep his word of honor. In contrast to the Pedro chronicle, where this kind of episode would be viewed as the cause of great troubles in the land, here the complaints are a matter of personal reputation.

Moralizing in the Chronicle of Juan I

There are several occasions in the chronicle of Juan I when the chronicler expresses disagreement with the king's plans or even with his course of action. For example, when Juan claimed the Portuguese throne after the death of King Ferrando of Portugal, Ayala comments that not all the members of the council were pleased, and some wished that he had first attempted to know more about the will of the Portuguese people in this matter. Later, the entire council opposed the monarch's plan to divide the kingdom and thereby make himself more acceptable as ruler of Portugal. It is the author's practice in this chronicle to express his point of view from within his role as a member of the royal council. Other judgments regarding the wisdom of certain decisions are more clearly grounded in the chancellor's moral stance. After Juan I decided that Clement VII was the true pope, Ayala reports that many felt that he should not have declared in favor of either pope. They believed that if all the kings maintained their neutrality, the schism in the church would not last so long.

On another occasion, the prelates of the kingdom complained to the king that certain laymen were collecting tithes due to the church, especially in the areas of Vizcaya, Alava, and Guipúzcoa. Part of the response contains a scathing denunciation of the prelates and the conditions and customs of the clergy. After acknowledging that the church may be more honored because of the great estates the prelates and clergy have, the chronicler points out the power they possess. Besides the tithes, they have cities, towns, castles, inheritances, vassals, and every sort of temporal jurisdiction. Since the Bible permitted the clergy to receive nothing more than tithes, the prevailing situation seems dishonest. Ayala adds: "And now, Sir, they want it all, for besides the temporal possessions that they have, they want to have the tithes. And, Sir, for the prelates to have such temporal wealth is very contrary to the service of God, of the churches and of their own persons. For this reason they spend their time in the houses of the kings and in the *cortes,* failing to attend to and visit their churches and those entrusted to them, not knowing how they live and what they are doing, so that many clerics, (a terrible sin!), because of not being visited nor examined, do not know how to consecrate the Body of God, nor do they live honestly" (BAE, 139).

When Juan I sought the advice of the lay members of his council in the problem of what to do with his troublesome half-brother Alfonso, the chronicler gives examples of actions by previous Castilian monarchs which serve as lessons in what should *not* be done. The tone of this passage recalls the moral judgments expressed in the chronicle of Pedro I. Ayala begins his counsel to the king in this way: "Sir, I have thought about this problem that you have told to the members of your council concerning the matter of Count Don Alfonso. And since I see great dangers in it, I would not wish, for anything in the world, that you go against God, nor against your reputation; rather I would want you to consider all the dangers that might come to you. And this reasoning is lauded and praised by all wise men, for a man should first suffer any danger whatsoever, even though it might be death, which is the harshest danger possible, rather than do an evil or ugly thing" (BAE, 95). The situation is especially sensitive because although Juan himself has the reputation of being a man who fears God and loves justice, some of his royal ancestors have, by their actions, damaged their reputations and done themselves great disservice. A deplorable result of this is that "all the kings of Christians talk about it, saying that the kings of Castile, violently and precipitously, killed some great persons of their kingdom in their palaces and without any manner of justice" (BAE, 95). Among the kings given as examples are Alfonso X, his son Sancho, Alfonso XI, and Pedro I. Although the chronicler's conclusion that "all this harm and evil have happened because such killings as these were done" (BAE, 96) is reminiscent of similar statements in the Pedro chronicle, the moral condemnation is accompanied by the additional concern for proceeding in a way that will ensure justice for the accused and preserve the good reputation of the king. Ayala does not condemn the deaths themselves so much as the covert procedures that denied a fair establishment of guilt or innocence. This judgmental passage is particularly interesting because of the explicit inclusion of the author's didactic considerations. It is also notable that the crimes of Pedro I are stated in a balanced way; in fact, much more detail is included in recounting the events during the reign of Alfonso XI.

Division but Not Despair

Ayala's moral-didactic message is evident throughout the chronicle of Enrique III, although not as directly stated as in his other chronicles. The depth of his concern is evident as he discusses the divisions at the highest levels of government and society which left no region or social class unaffected. This is reflected in the following representative examples:

and with all this, the aforementioned tutors never were in agreement among themselves, and therefore the common benefit and good was often forgotten. (BAE, 196)

And the knights of the kingdom, since they saw such disorder, did not care about anything, and everything was robbed. . . . (BAE, 179)

And for this reason there were deaths and fights in many places, and those who were more powerful expelled others from the city or town where they were and they took the king's money, and there was little agreement and obedience in the whole realm, and many disturbances and much discord. (BAE, 178)

Thus, because of these things, much damage increased in the city [Seville], and many disturbances; but later it was the will of God that all were friends and reached an agreement. (BAE, 197)

There is repeated insistence on the ideas of greed, self-centeredness, and lawlessness, which result in chaos and grave damage to the realm. During the negotiations with the duke of Benavente, in an effort to prevent his marriage to the daughter of the Portuguese king, there is continued stress on trying to get the duke to do what is in the king's service and to the duke's honor.

One of the rare actions that merits praise is the effort of the people of Burgos to arrange to hold the Cortes in their city. Ayala is impressed by their selflessness, even to the point of offering their own sons as security. He comments: "and all this was done very well and at great cost to the city of Burgos, in order to serve the king and the kingdom" (BAE, 181). Even though the chancellor perceives the reality of life in which human actions are dominated by an unbridled zeal for material profit, it is apparent that he still believes in the chivalric standards of behavior and the spiritual values of liberality, rectitude, and loyalty. If these were practiced, it would result in order, harmony, and mutual concern. Not only were there few persons in Spain at the time who represented these ideals, but the great figures of Europe, like Charles V of France, Edward III of England, the Black Prince, Bertrand Du Guesclin, and the duke of Lancaster had also disappeared.[3]

The Gallant Knights: Reality and Symbol

In the other chronicles, however, Ayala clearly demonstrates his preoccupation with moral-didactic matters by using examples of persons who possess lofty chivalric ideals. In the case of Pedro I, the chivalric qualities of the king's adversaries often contrast markedly with the less favorable characteristics attributed to Pedro himself.[4] Being a representative of the noble class, Pero López feels and aspires to these idealistic values. There is no doubt that he admires figures like the Black Prince, Alfonso Ferrández Coronel, the marshall of Audrehem, and Bertrand Du Guesclin, all deeply concerned with their honor and reputation. For example, during the siege of Aguilar, when Pedro's forces succeeded in battering down one of the portals of the city walls, many of the inhabitants surrendered. The exception was Ferrández Coronel, who insisted on remaining there and fighting to the death. Because of his distrust of Juan Alfonso de Alburquerque, Ferrández Coronel had rebelled against his lord the king, contravening the chivalric code. At the point of death, he reaffirmed his philosophy as a knight when he said: "Gutier Ferrández, friend, the recourse from here on is this: to die with as much dignity as I am able as a knight" (37). Then Ferrández Coronel put on his helmet, fastened on his sword, and went to hear mass and receive communion. Confused by what he perceived as a lapse in his lord's usual bravery, his squire asked him why he remained there instead of going out to fight alongside the others. Coronel embodied the virtue of deep Christian faith as he replied: "Regardless of what happens, first I will see God" (37).

Other chivalric virtues are evident in two similar examples that deal with the squire of Ferrández Coronel and with Arias Gómez de Silva, a Portuguese knight in the service of Juan I. The conduct of the two men affords us a model of fidelity and constancy. After defending the castle of his lord, the squire was captured and his hands were cut off as punishment for not surrendering the fortress to the king. Once his wounds had healed, he went to Aguilar where he asked permission from the king to be placed inside the town in order that he might die with his lord. Arias Gómez de Silva also presents an outstanding example of fidelity during the war of Portuguese succession. Arias Gómez had been the tutor of King Fernando of Portugal, and his wife, Doña Urraca Tenorio, was the governess of Beatriz of Portugal, second wife of Juan I. Arias Gómez was in charge of the Portuguese town and castle of Guimaranes when the master of Avis besieged the town, using every imaginable device against him. When Arias Gómez could no longer hold out against the day and night bombardment, he requested a forty-day period in which to send word to Castile, asking either for help to be sent or to be relieved of his pledge of homage. According to the knight's code of conduct, his only other recourse would be to die in defense of the castle. The response of Juan I reveals the great appreciation he felt for all that Gómez and his people had suffered in order to serve him. Unfortunately, it was impossible for the Castilian king to send help before the time period expired, although he was gathering his armies to enter Portugal and subdue the rebels. It was Juan's will that Arias Gómez not be lost, for he was worth much more to the king than were the town and castle. He therefore instructed the Portuguese knight to surrender so that he and his men would be safe and would soon be able to serve their lord again.

There are also some chivalric elements in the literary portrait of Doña Blanca de Borbón which is included in the chronicle of Pedro I after her death. Ayala is impressed by her aristocratic background as well as her characteristics and actions that are appropriate to a praiseworthy lady of noble rank. The sketch seems to be written from a very sympathetic point of view: "And this Queen Blanca was of the lineage of the king of France, of the fleur-de-lis of the Bourbons who have for arms a shield with fleurs-de-lis like the king of France, and a colored band across the shield. And she was at the age of twenty-five years when she died, and she was fair, blond, graceful and intelligent. And every day she said her prayers very devoutly, and she underwent great suffering in the prisons where she was and she endured it with great patience" (122).

Chivalry at the Battle of Nájera

It is not surprising that the most concentrated presence of chivalric elements in the chronicle of Pedro I is noted in the chapters that deal with the Battle of Nájera and the events that follow it. Ayala, standard bearer for Enrique II, describes in detail how the forces on each side were arranged. Referring to those who came with the Prince of Wales, the chronicler comments: "and these men of arms were then the flower of chivalry of Christendom, for there was peace then between France and England" (161). After a decisive victory, won with the help of his English allies, Pedro asked the Prince of Wales for the captives that he considered most dangerous. The Castilian king was surely confounded by the prince's refusal on chivalric grounds, stating that they must also consider the honor and purses of their captors.

The decision by the prince to allow the marshall of Audrehem to be judged by twelve of his peers contrasts sharply with the previous chapter, in which it is reported that Pedro ordered a number of prisoners put to death. The marshall was accused of being a traitor and of being disloyal by the Prince of Wales, who said he should be killed. According to the prince, after the marshall had been taken prisoner in the Battle of Piteus, the prince not only assessed a very small ransom but also released his prisoner on his word of honor without paying the ransom. The marshall had pledged homage to the prince and vowed that until such time as the ransom were paid, he would not fight against the English king or against the prince unless the king of France or a member of the French royal family in person were in the battle. The marshall responded to the prince's accusation in an extremely courteous and respectful manner, saying: "Sir, with humble reverence I ask you if it pleases you to say anything more against me in this matter that you have spoken of before these knights whom you have ordered in this dispute." After the prince's negative reply, the old knight continued: " 'Sir, I beg of you not to be angry with me because I speak of my right, for this matter touches my reputation and my word of honor.' And the prince said that surely he should speak of it, for this was a matter of knights and war, and it was right for each one to defend his reputation and his word of honor" (165–66). The marshall defended himself by saying that since Pedro was paying the English salaries, he, and not the prince, was in charge of the battle. Therefore, the marshall was fighting against Pedro and not against the Prince of Wales. The chronicler reports that the prince and all the knights were very pleased that, by his sound reasoning, he had excused himself, because he was and always had been a good knight.

Another exemplary knight is Bertrand Du Guesclin, who was also taken prisoner by the Prince of Wales in the Battle of Nájera. Whereas the marshall of Audrehem exemplifies the attributes of courtesy, loyalty, and honor, Du Guesclin typifies the brave and famous warrior. Ayala states that it would have pleased the prince if Sir Bertrand had died in battle because he was such a warlike knight. Nevertheless, the prince treated his prisoner with great honor. Since Du Guesclin was "a very great and very good knight," and in view of the fact that England and France were at war, the prince decided to forego the ransom money and keep the French knight prisoner. When the latter learned of this decision, he said to the prince's messenger: "Tell my lord the Prince that I hold that God and he grant me a very great favor, among many other honors that I have had in this world of chivalry, that my lance should be so feared that I lie in prison during the wars between France and England, and for no other reason. And since it is thus, I consider my imprisonment more honorable than my deliverance. And [tell him] that he may be certain that I consider it a signal grace, for all who hear and know of it will feel that I receive great honor from this; and the good and the glory of chivalry consists of this, for life swiftly passes" (168).

The prince, realizing that Sir Bertrand was right, tried to trick him into setting a low ransom price for himself. He instructed his messenger: "If he promises a single wisp of straw in exchange for himself, for that I'll grant him his freedom" (168). Sir Bertrand immediately saw that the prince was trying to lessen his honor, and replied: "I am a knight poor in gold and coins, but with the efforts of my friends, I will give him 100,000 gold francs for my body . . ." (168). In response to his letters, his friends, the powerful knights of Brittany, sent their squires bearing their seals and the power to oblige them to pay whatever quantity Du Guesclin wished for his ransom. Ayala mentions the seals six times and comments: "And in France and England, the greatest obligation that a knight can give to a noble is his seal; for they say that for a man to sign his name is a great deal, but in the seal goes the name and the coat of arms, which are the honor of the knight" (169). When the king of France later learned what had happened, he not only paid the complete ransom, relieving Du Guesclin's friends from their pledges, but further honored his vassal by giving him an additional thirty thousand francs for clothing, equipment, horse, and armor. Ayala ends his narration of this episode with a rather lengthy exposition of his didactic message, concluding that "for all these reasons this story was put here, for there is great reason for the generosity, nobility, and donations of kings to remain in the memory, and not be forgotten. Furthermore [it shows] the good motives of chivalry" (169). This conclusion is a reaffirmation of the purposes presented earlier in the prologue.

An Exemplary Knight: Enrique II

There is evidence of the author's moral-didactic purpose throughout the chronicle, but this sort of reinforcing statement appears more frequently toward the end of the chronicle of Pedro I. During the years from 1366 to 1369, Pedro I and Enrique II both claimed the throne of Castile and Leon. Although the chronicler cannot change the events that occurred, it seems apparent that he attempts to portray Enrique as another exemplary chivalric knight. Pedro is not even mentioned as a participant in the chapter dealing with the battle of Nájera. On the other hand, Enrique, the vanquished, is presented as a valiant knight who fulfills the lord's duty to aid and defend his vassals. Before the battle, the French advised him not to fight because of the high quality of the English men-at-arms. Nevertheless, Enrique had to prove that, regardless of the dangers, he would not desert his people, in contrast to Pedro, who had left the citizens of Burgos defenseless some months earlier. Ayala describes Enrique's role in the battle this way: "And King Enrique arrived two or three times on his horse, armed with a lorica, to aid his men who were on foot, believing that all of his mounted men who were with him would do the same. And he arrived where he saw that his banner was, for it had not yet been torn down, and when he arrived in the press of battle and saw that his men were not fighting, he had to turn back, for he could not resist the enemy because they were very forceful . . ." (164). Rather than viewing the defeat as the will of God, and therefore a judgment against Enrique, Ayala attributes it to the caliber of the English knights and the flight of Enrique's brother Tello and his company.

The Spanish historian Luis Suárez Fernández attributes the eventual Trastámara victory over Pedro to two distinct factors: the rebellion of the nobility against Pedro I and the decisive aid of Charles V of France. The nobles considered Enrique to be the representative of their ideals and the defender and rebuilder of the nobility.[5] His alliance with the

French, who since the time of Saint Louis represented the chivalric spirit in Europe, lent further support to a system of aristocratic predominance. This fact also made it easier for Ayala to present Enrique II as the embodiment of chivalric ideals, while showing Pedro, at the end of his reign, as the antithesis of these ideals. In his last analysis of Pedro's reign, Ayala stresses the moral issue once more: "And he killed many in his kingdom, because of which all the harm that you have heard of came to him. And therefore we will say here what the prophet David said: 'Now let the kings learn and all those who judge the world be advised—for a great and marvelous judgment was this, and very frightful' " (198). Contrast this with the idealized picture of Enrique II contained in the pope's letter to Juan I after the latter's defeat at Aljubarrota: "And you know well that that noble chosen one among the noble men of chivalry, and knight above all knights, who in the dangers of death showed his great force, the King Don Enrique, your father, was defeated: remember that" (BAE, 109).

Piety and Pageantry

Juan I also serves Ayala very well as a representative of another chivalric ideal: the Christian monarch. Early in Juan's reign, the king of Armenia sent out letters to all the Christian kings, seeking their help in freeing him from the prison of the sultan of Babilonia. Juan's reaction is one of *piedad,* that is, pity, compassion, or piety. According to the chronicle, the Armenian king was freed mainly through the efforts of Juan I. In the letters from the sultan and his advisor, the Castilian king is addressed in such chivalric terms as "exalted, esteemed, valiant, the knight of honor, the lion, defender of Christianity, honorer of the people of Jesus, crown of the law of Christ, defender against enemies, insurer of the people of the Cross, maker of knights, beauty of nobilities and of chronicles" and "a just person" *(justiciero)* (BAE, 82).[6] Throughout his reign, Juan I is viewed as a devout man, interested in the welfare of the church. He founded monasteries and encouraged monastic and clerical reforms. Shortly before his death, the young king established two new orders of chivalry. These two orders illustrate the major aspects of chivalry present in the chronicle: the religious and the symbolic or heraldic. The Order of the Holy Spirit had as its emblem a white dove on a chain that resembled the rays of the sun. The second order initiated by Juan I is the Order of the Rose, its emblem to be worn by the king's squires in jousts and tourneys.

Other episodes occur in this chronicle that also demonstrate the interest that the king and the chronicler had in the pageantry of chivalry and in its symbolic value. Juan began his reign with an elaborate celebration and coronation ceremony. The Castilian custom was for the heir to the throne to become king immediately following the death of the previous king. At that time, a coronation ceremony was a novelty in Castile. Juan's coronation was held in Burgos on 25 July, Saint James's day, in order to recall the fact that the king had received his quality of knighthood directly from the warrior saint, patron of Spain. On the same day, Juan himself initiated one hundred men of the realm into knighthood. Similar celebrations were held in many other towns, where the king was represented by his coat of arms during the contests and dances.

In the Cortes of Guadalajara in 1390, the king established an inheritance and a coat of arms for his second son, the Infante Ferrando. The heraldic emblems and coats of arms were used by the crusaders to identify themselves on battlefields far from home. The decoration on the shield originally represented heroic deeds in battle. In this case, the arms of the young prince symbolize his royal lineage and his domain. They consisted of a shield with a castle and a lion on the right side, because he was the legitimate son of Juan I. On the left appeared the arms of the king of Aragon, his grandfather. The border of the shield contained artificial figures representing the seigniory of Lara. The king also crowned his son with a wreath of pearls, naming him duke of Peñafiel. A charming scene follows in which the two little princes formally thank the king, their father, for the mercies bestowed on Ferrando. The younger boy then pledged his fealty to his brother. This caused many who were present to remark that if there were more like him in the realm, it would be a great defense for the kingdom.

Because of the disastrous results of military campaigns and the death of many experienced knights during the reign of Juan I, Ayala had to look to France for examples of chivalric conduct in battle. These episodes bear little resemblance to any other battle scenes in the chronicles. The author here concentrates on pageantry rather than strategy or battle formations. In the first episode, Charles VI of France went to the aid of the count of Flanders. The king was accompanied by six thousand men of arms, among whom there were three dukes, twenty-two counts, and one hundred and twenty banners of French grandees. Ayala was one of the eleven knights who rode alongside and served as guards for the thirteen-year-old monarch. He notes that, because the king was so young and so small, he rode a small horse and wore no spurs—an important symbol of knighthood. The French were outnumbered in the battle—some manuscripts indicate that there were 80,000 men of Flanders, of whom 26,000 died, others say there were 8,000 with 6,000 casualties. In either case, the French victory is attributed to their excellence rather than their numbers. They suffered the loss of only twenty-six men. The king accorded great honor to those who died. When he left Flanders, he took with him the bodies of his dead knights, covered with cloths of gold. To further honor them, after the funeral mass, he gave money to build a chapel where they would be buried. In the second episode, no battle occurs. It is apparent that the chronicler's main purpose is to describe the impressive panorama of the French king majestically commanding a force of 22,000 men of arms. Among the group of fully armed knights were eight dukes, thirty-six counts, and three hundred and sixty standards of grandees. Ayala also adds that of the 22,000, 14,000 were squires of honor and 8,000 were knights of the highest category, as symbolized by their golden spurs.

Dates and Details

Ayala's concern with chivalric conduct does not deter him from including an abundance of detail even in the most idealistic scenes mentioned above. Careful, convincing description, filled with specific details, contributes a great deal to the impression of verisimilitude in the chronicles and is characteristic of Ayala's method of narration. The division of the chronicles into years and chapters represents an effort at logical arrangement of data and seems to situate the author outside of the material as an observer and coordinator rather than inventor. Specific dates are often included in the narration. For example, when referring to an important occasion in the life of Alfonso XI, the chronicler is exceedingly specific: "And this battle before the town of Tarifa took place on Monday, the thirtieth day of October, in the year of the birth of our Lord Jesus Christ 1340, and in the era of Cesar 1378, and [the year] of the creation of the world according to the count of the Hebrews 5110 and in the year of the Arabs 742" (13). In chapter 1 of the second year of Pedro's reign, Ayala comments on his intention to begin each year by stating the date according to the different methods of computation. He includes a long and thorough explanation of this system of dating and the historical background for each method.[7]

Dates are commonly supplied throughout the chronicles, but they are not usually so comprehensive; for example, referring to the death of the brother of Doña María de Padilla, "they defeated and overcame Don Juan García, and they killed him in the fight: which was Friday, the twenty-seventh day of November of this year" (76). The dates of births or deaths generally include the date and month, and often the day of the week, as in the preceding example. Sometimes the saint's day is mentioned in addition to the date or is substituted for it. Preparations were being made prior to the Battle of Aljubarrota the "eve of Saint Mary of August, Monday, the fourteenth day of the month of this year" (BAE, 102). Juan I was crowned on Saint James's day, 1379, and the duke of Lancaster arrived at La Coruña to begin his invasion of Castile on the same saint's day in 1386. Religious seasons such as Carnaval (Shrovetide) and Lent are also used to date events; for example, the king of Navarre visited Juan I and "was with him several days enjoying himself during Carnaval" (BAE, 118). Sometimes a general time reference is given, such as "in the beginning of this year," "in the beginning of the summer," or, referring to the truce with Portugal, "they were proclaimed in the middle of the month of May" (BAE, 209). Because there are fewer specific events and more extended discussions and negotiations in the chronicle of Enrique III, this sort of general reference tends to occur more often. Occasionally, when one would expect more specificity, the chronicler is unaccountably vague: "and it was ordered that on a certain day Doña Catalina would come to Castile" (BAE, 120). In contrast, the day that Enrique III had the duke of Benavente arrested, a great deal of information is given: "And thus it was that one Saturday, Saint James' day, the twenty-fifth of July, in the afternoon, in Burgos . . ." (BAE, 228). Events like this, which are described in a more dramatic fashion, tend to include more data in regard to specific dates and times.

Long lists of the names of knights who participated in various battles, or who were present at meetings, not only testify to the exactness of the chronicler, but also record and praise noble participants. The latter no doubt represent a large part of the public to which Ayala directed his chronicles. Particularly dealing with the factious reigns of Pedro I and Enrique III, some of the lists serve to point out advocates of one or another position or alliance. During the reign of Enrique II, the lists often indicate the lands that the king distributed among the Castilian nobles who joined him, or the possessions given to pay for the services of the French mercenaries. At the beginning of Juan's effort to take over the throne of Portugal, the chronicler enumerates the Portuguese towns and knights who allied themselves with the Castilian king. He also names the many important nobles who died of the plague during the siege of Lisbon.

The Traveling Monarchs

Other details that lend authenticity to the chronicles are place names and geographical features mentioned during journeys, and frequent inclusion of numbers referring to different types of troops, distances, and time of day. The abundance of this sort of information in the chronicle of Pedro I reflects the great mobility and extraordinary velocity used by the monarch.[8] Pedro personally commanded the numerous campaigns against the Aragonese, in which mobility and surprise attack were characteristic strategies. Whether a threat existed to the kingdom or to his own authority, on land or on sea, Pedro was a very able military leader who went in person to every point of conflict. The seizure of the city of Tarazona is an effective example of a detailed scene dominated by the monarch: "When the King Don Pedro was in Deza, a town of his on the border of Aragon, he found out that the city of Tarazona, which belongs to the king of Aragon, was a good city with a lot of food. It was not strongly walled, there were few people in it, and it was near there. The king left Deza for Agreda. And on the next day he left there for Tarazona, and on the way he took a castle that belonged to the king of Aragon, which they called Santa Cruz, and from there he went directly to Tarazona. And the day that he arrived there was Thursday, 9 March of this year, and he took the city of Tarazona by force, and entered through the section of the Moorish quarter, which was weak . . ." (86).

Some of Pedro's travel was due to his pursuit of enemies, or at times to his desire to return to María de Padilla. For example, shortly after his wedding to Blanca de Borbón, the young king hurriedly left Valladolid and "went that day to sleep in a place called Pajares, which is a village beyond Olmedo, sixteen leagues from Valladolid: and the next day he went to Puebla de Montalbán where Doña María de Padilla was. For although he had left her in the castle of Montalván, he had already sent word to her to come to Puebla de Montalván, which is two leagues closer, and there he found her" (42). Within a few days, Juan Alfonso de Alburquerque decided to follow the king and try to convince him to return. After naming some of the 1,500 mounted men who accompanied him, the towns on his route are listed: "he went to some villages near Olmedo; and the next day, Thursday, he went from there to sleep in Parraces. And the next day, Friday, he went to eat at Espinar de Segovia, and to sleep at Felipal. And the next day, Saturday, he went to eat and sleep at Sant Martin de Valde Iglesias. Sunday he went to Almorox, a village of Escalona" (43). An impression of urgency is created by the repetition of the same phrases, the names of the days of the week, and the same preterite tense verb "he went." The effectiveness of these lines is heightened by their location at the end of the chapter, and also by the fact that the next chapter begins with the news that at midnight that same day the king's messenger arrived.

In both the chronicles of Pedro I and Enrique II, there are many examples of the king's going from one place to another. In the case of Juan I, however, one notices that although the king is reported to be in many different locations, the chronicler more often begins by saying, "while the king was in. . . ." This technique tends to remove the emphasis from the motion and focus it on the event that is occurring or on the problem under discussion. This, of course, affects the tone of the chronicle itself. The chronicle of Enrique III is, for the most part, static. This is reflected even in the external structure of the work. The chronological units, that is, year and chapter divisions, are generally much longer than those in the other three chronicles. Debate and negotiation predominate over action. Because of the youth of the king, he is not an active, dynamic figure. Some sense of movement is supplied by the travels of others, particularly the archbishop of Toledo and the duke of Benavente. However, once the king's majority has been declared, the tempo increases as he confronts members of his family. Numbers are often quoted in this chronicle to reflect the relative strengths of two opposing groups. The mention of the build-up of forces on each side is one technique used to create an element of tension.

The visit of Enrique III to Vizcaya in 1393, to be received as lord of the territory, is one of the most interesting episodes in any of the chronicles in terms of abundance of place names and geographical features, as well as description of the land and customs. The law of Vizcaya required that the king, or whoever was to receive the seigniory, had to personally go there. The king went with only a few companies because "the land is not supplied with food, and it is rough and uneven terrain" (BAE, 212). When the small entourage reached Bilbao, letters were sent out summoning the Basque knights to the place where they were accustomed to meet. The next day the king arrived at "a sierra that in Basque they call Arechabalaga, which in the language of Castile means Wide Oak" (BAE, 213). All the area nobles, along with their companies, had already gathered there to present their petitions to the king. As a symbol of their acceptance of Enrique as their lord, they all kissed his hand, and then asked him to swear to keep their laws and privileges. According to Basque law, this had to be done in a church about two miles away called Larrabezúa. The king went to the church, "entered within, and made the aforementioned oath on the altar. And he ate there that day, and went to sleep in a town they call Garnica . . ." (BAE, 213). The king continued to observe the Basque traditions as he traveled to Bermeo, on the seashore. The following day he went to hear mass in a church called Santa Ofemia, where the Lords of Vizcaya usually took an oath to uphold the privileges of that town and area. The ceremony of the oath and a disagreement between the king and the people are described in some detail. Before leaving Vizcaya, Enrique consulted with his advisors concerning the problems of the area. He then issued his decision "standing near a great oak where the magistrates of Vizcaya usually judge and the Lords of Vizcaya order their laws" (BAE, 214). The king went from there to Durango and the next day to Victoria, "a very good city that the king has in Alava" (BAE, 214). The journey continued as the group proceeded to Burgos, but did not stay there as there was illness in the city at the time. Several more cities are enumerated before the king finally reached the forests of Segovia, where he rested before returning to Madrid to preside over the Cortes.

Although Ayala is not named as one of the nobles who accompanied the young monarch to Vizcaya, it is likely that he was present since he was one of the most powerful Basque nobles. The passage reflects local traditions and a number of the legal customs of the region. Ayala's interest in and knowledge of his home area is apparent in a number of other references to Basque towns, weather, and terrain scattered through the chronicles:

And then Don Tello fled to Vizcaya, and arrived at Bermeo, a town of his on the shores of the sea. And as soon as he arrived, he entered the fishing boats and went to a place near Bayonne called San Juan de Luz. . . . And from there [Aguilar de Campo] the king [Pedro] went to Vizcaya and arrived in Bermeo the day that Don Tello had entered the sea, which was Thursday, 7 May of this year. And the king entered other ships and went out to sea, trying to overtake him. And he arrived at a place on the coast called Lequeçio, and the sea was a little rough. (92)

King Don Enrique made his way through the land of Guipúzcoa to lay siege to the city of Bayonne, as it was arranged. And since it was summer, around Saint John's day, there was a lot of water, so much so that many horses and beasts were lost in that land of Guipúzcoa, which is very harsh. And the army of the king was very short of food, for in that land it was not available: for one reason because of the great waters and for another reason because the land of Guipúzcoa is isolated from where the food is. (BAE, 23)

And while the king [Juan] was in Burgos during Lent, he got sick. And after he felt better, he left Burgos for Vitoria to continue on his way from there to Fuenterrabia. . . . And his doctors told him it was not in his interests to leave there, for the land of Guipúzcoa, where he was to go, was very difficult to travel through. Besides, it was winter, and there were still snow storms and floods, and he was not ready for this effort. (BAE, 123).

Terrain and Weather

There are a few other references to terrain or weather conditions in other parts of the Peninsula, for example, the harsh countryside near Avila or the cold in Gijón that caused changes in royal plans. At times these aspects of nature are determining factors in military efforts. Ayala refers to the effect of unusual April weather on Pedro's troops: "And that day it was terribly hot, and there was great thirst in the king's army, and some foot soldiers died of thirst . . ." (86). On another occasion, Pedro was leading the attack on an Aragonese town when most of his ships were destroyed by a storm at sea. Ayala describes the episode this way: "at midday, a very strong wind came up in the sea, which is a crosswind in that region and very dangerous weather. And as the ships were without people to control them, the wind blew the ships crossways to the coast, so that the eighteen ships of the king and of the Genoese all wrecked on the land, except two galleys, one of the king and another of the Genoese, which were farther out to sea" (94). The siege of Ciudad Rodrigo by Enrique II failed because of winter conditions. After describing the great efforts made to break through the city walls, the chronicler concludes: "but the winter rains were so great that he could not continue the assault on the city, nor could any food reach him from anywhere because of the great waters and harsh winter weather; therefore he could not stay there any longer" (BAE, 5). The soldiers of Juan I were defeated at Troncoso in 1385 because of the disarray that resulted from a long march and "the great heat that there was, for it was the month of July, and, because the land was plowed, there was a great amount of dust . . ." (BAE, 99). These short passages have a certain austerity not only because of the kind of conditions they describe, but also due to the repetition of a restricted number of adjectives: "great," "much," "harsh," or "difficult." Ayala does not include nature descriptions for variety or embellishment. The emphasis is clearly on the result of the particular weather or terrain described.

A somewhat different style and purpose prevails in the passage describing the duke of Benavente's effort to carry out a surprise seizure of Zamora during the reign of Enrique III. The description of the dense fog and the frustrated attempt to reach the city deftly conveys the impression of aimless wandering. The chronicler relates that "the fog was so great all night that they could not stay on the road, for whenever they neared Zamora, they went back again where they came from: and thus they wandered lost all night because of the fog" (é la niebla fué tan grande toda la noche, que non podian tener tiento al camino, que cuando estaban cerca de Zamora, otra vez se tornaban á do venian: é asi anduvieron perdidos toda la noche con la niebla") (BAE, 204). The sentence begins and ends with the words "fog," "all night," and a verb in the preterite tense, indicating a restricted time frame. The middle of the sentence, however, contains four verbs in the imperfect tense, indicating the repetitiveness of their actions. The placement of two of these verbs on either side of the name of the town reflects their coming and going and reinforces the impression of the futility of their repeated efforts to reach their objective. This is a particularly effective technique at this point in the chronicle, for this action represents the anticlimactic end of the duke's threat to the power of the monarchy.

Personal Observations

Occasionally the chronicler also includes brief descriptions of cities, towns, and castles. Sometimes the comments suggest the author's personal observations. When Pedro I had difficulty taking the tower of the bridge of Toro, Ayala remarks that it was a wonder that it could be defended that long, for the tower was a small, low fortress. Another time, after the troops of Enrique II set fire to the Rua Nova in Lisbon, Ayala regretfully observes that it was the most beautiful street in the city. A frequent motive for this type of description is to point out strategic importance. For example, when the Moors recaptured Algeciras during the reign of Enrique II, the chronicler discusses the city's importance to all of Castile, but especially to Andalusia, "for it was a great sea port and a well supplied place, for it had Portugal on one side and Aragon on the other side . . ." (BAE, 4). In the chronicle of Enrique III, the king's tutors arranged for him to go to Segovia "because it is a good city, and it is in the middle of the kingdom" (BAE, 197). In 1393, Enrique III received interesting news of an expedition to the Canary Islands by explorers from Seville, Vizcaya, and Guipúzcoa. The report contains such details as the fact that they took horses on the ships, the names and measurements of all the islands, and the people and materials they brought back. The message ends with the observation that if the king wishes, it would be easy to conquer the islands and at very little cost.

There are many other examples of detailed descriptions that contribute to the effectiveness and realistic quality of the narration. They also seem to admit the possibility of observation or participation by the chronicler himself, recalling Ayala's words in his prologue. It is known that the young Pero López attended the wedding of Pedro I and Blanca de Borbón in 1353. His description reflects such customs and observations as the prenuptial vigil of the couple, the selection of wedding attendants, and the procession with participants mounted on horses or on mules, with the bridal couple riding white horses. He also mentions the entourage of each one including their names, the rich wedding attire of the bride and groom, and the jousts and tourneys that followed the wedding.

Military Campaigns

During the half century of his involvement in court circles, Ayala participated in many of the military campaigns carried out by Pedro I, Enrique II, and Juan I. He was so knowledgeable that during the latter's reign he served as military advisor to the king of France. He includes in the chronicles a wide variety of battle descriptions, ranging from the mere statement that certain places were taken, to fully detailed accounts of plans, battle order, and the combat itself. At times the chronicler records the capture of towns or castles without mentioning the battle that was involved. This news is often included in a chapter where the siege or capture of another place is described. For example, in 1369, after an unsuccessful attempt to take the city of Guimaranes, the chapter ends with the single statement that "the King Don Enrique took the town and castle of Breganza that he had surrounded, and left a contingent there and headed for Castile" (BAE, 4). In another case, after the Battle of Aljubarrota, there are details regarding the capture of Santarem by the master of Avis, followed by the report that "then he captured all the fortresses that the King Don Juan had in that region . . ." (BAE, 106).

Sometimes battles are mentioned and only sparse details supplied. Usually the numbers on each side and the victor are noted. The Moorish attack on Murcia in 1392 is an event of great potential interest that is described only briefly. The chronicler reports that in spite of a truce between Granada and Castile, a Moorish army of 700 mounted men and 3,000 foot soldiers invaded Murcia, saying that they wanted to try out Christian lands. The governor of Murcia, with 170 cavalry and 400 infantrymen, "fought with them, and defeated them and killed many of them . . ." (BAE, 201). The brief chapter ends by stating the name of the governor. Quite often the chronicler mentions sieges of towns and the standard devices used. The description of the assault on Aguilar contains more details than usual: "After King Don Pedro had laid siege to the town of Aguilar for four months, he took it by force, preparing tunnels and excavations, in this manner. Thursday, the first of February, they set fire to the excavations they had made, and a large part of the wall fell. Many from the town came out through there and joined the king. And the next day, Friday, the king ordered all the men of his army to be armed in order to fight against the town, and they did it this way" (37).

Battle Strategy and Psychology

There are a number of incidents of moderate extension and importance that are considerably more developed, and include motives and strategy as well as details of preparation and execution. Two of these episodes are related to the struggles between Pedro I and the nobility, especially his half-brothers. The people of Toledo had rebelled against the king because of the detention of Queen Blanca in their city. This supplied the perfect opportunity for the nobles to join in the uprising against Pedro which resulted in his imprisonment in Toro. Although the nobles insisted that the motive for their actions was to serve and honor the king, it was apparent that their real concern was to remove the Padilla family from power and redistribute their possessions and offices among themselves. The first of these incidents involves the efforts of the nobles to agree among themselves and to coordinate their resistance to the king. Chapter 25 of the year 1354 provides a good example of Ayala's ability to increase interest in the narration by taking a relatively simple event and using it to create dramatic tension. The chapter begins with a brief two-sentence reminder of the alliance of the king's half-brother Enrique, Ferrando de Castro, and Juan Alfonso de Alburquerque and of Enrique's trip to Asturias to bring back foot soldiers. A sense of urgency and movement during their rapid journey from Salas to Villalón is achieved by the specific mention of each of the four days that passes, by reference to time of day, and by naming the town where they ate and slept, as well as the bridges they crossed. This impression is particularly enhanced by the series of eight preterite verbs, in short phrases stressing motion:

and they went that day to sleep at Val de San Lorenzo. And the next day, Thursday, they crossed the bridge of Astorga, and went to sleep at the bridge of Orvego. And the next day, Friday, they went toward Valencia, and they went to eat at Nava, a village two leagues from Mayorga. And they left there in the afternoon, and at night they passed through Mayorga. And when the next day, Saturday, dawned, they were at the gate of Villalon. . . .

e fueron esse dia dormir a Val de Sannd Llorençio. E otro dia jueues pasaron por la puente de Astorga e fueron dormir a la puente de Oruego. E otro dia viernes fueron camino de Valençia e fueron comer a Naua, vna aldea dos leguas de Mayorga, e de alli partieron en la tarde e pasaron de noche por Mayorga. E quando amanesçio otro dia sabado estauan a la puente de Villalon. . . . (58)

A change of rhythm is signaled by the switch to imperfect tense verbs. In addition, the next sentence begins with a dependent clause, followed by two more verbs in the imperfect tense. All of these combine to slow the pace of the action. This sentence contains news that halts the progress of Enrique and the others: the infantes of Aragon and Don Tello have joined forces and are in the nearby town of Cuenca de Tamariz with a sizable army.

Because they do not know the intention of the infantes and Tello, the possibility exists that a battle is imminent. The final portion of the chapter consists of five sentences, each dealing with a certain phase of the preparation for armed confrontation. The action of the first and last sentences takes place on the hill facing the city. At first, three horsemen are stationed there as lookouts, and at the end all of Enrique's forces are aligned in battle formation on the crest of the hill. The second and fourth lines are identical in structure, and both describe precise preparations being made. Details such as the following are especially effective in producing a visual image of the action: "And they ordered that everyone eat and give feed to the horses in some threshing areas that were there, for it was in the month of August," and "they ordered that everyone mount up and put on their battle helmets" (58). The scene would have been more vivid, with an even greater sense of activity, if the chronicler had used the indicative mood rather than the subjunctive, which in this case seems to move the reader a step farther away from the event. The central focus of the passage is in the third line, which gives a strong impression of urgency by beginning with a time reference "in barely an hour," followed by the verbs "he came" and "he said." One of the sentinels reports that "fifty mounted horsemen were coming out of Cuenca, their lances in their hands, and they were coming toward them at full speed" (58). The uncertainty about the other group's intention now is dramatically resolved by the reference to the swift and menacing approach of the armed horsemen. The atmosphere of tension and apprehension continues unabated as Ayala ends the chapter with a vivid picture of the battle flags, horsemen, and foot soldiers poised for the encounter. This brief episode is not of major importance in the progress of the narration, occurring as it does between two of the most vital and dramatic events in the chronicle (the Toledo uprising and the Toro episode). This fact makes even more impressive the evidence of conscious stylistic arrangement of detail for maximum effect on the audience.

The other episode involves a confrontation between Pedro I and his half-brothers Enrique and Fadrique. Several months after Pedro's escape from Toro, they found themselves in the extremely dangerous position of being the only remnant still opposed to the king. When the brothers learned that Pedro was in a town less than twenty miles from Toledo, they rushed to arrive there before the king. There is a great disparity between their real reasons for going to Toledo and the altruistic statements they made to the people. According to Enrique and Fadrique, they were afraid that if the king entered the city, the queen and the townspeople would suffer. Therefore, they insisted that "they came there to help them and to be with them in order to aid them" (70), upholding the oaths they had made. The Toledans were fully aware of the probable consequences if they acceded to the wishes of the two nobles. In a very courteous and diplomatic manner, they thanked the brothers for coming, saying that it appeared that they come to help. Nevertheless, when it became apparent that most of the nobles had stopped supporting the queen's cause, the people sent messengers to try to arrange a solution with the king. If they allowed Count Enrique and his brother to enter Toledo, "which was the king's city, and such a strong and noble place" (71), it would destroy their negotiations with the king. Instead of welcoming them, they requested that the brothers return to Talavera, where they would send them news of what happened. Enrique and Fadrique were very discontent and unconvinced by the citizens' logic. The following day, some who favored the two nobles let them secretly enter the city by way of another bridge. The chronicler reveals the brothers' true motives when he comments that it was a good thing for them that they were allowed to enter, "for they did not have any agreement with the king, nor did they trust him, and they wanted to take possession of such a good city as Toledo in whatever manner possible . . ." (71). Although some within the city joined the nobles, others took refuge in the *alcazar*. The chapter ends with the observation that "then there was a very great disturbance in the whole city" (71).

The second chapter of this incident begins with two strange pieces of information. First, Fadrique is criticized in a manner reminiscent of the many condemnations leveled against Pedro I. The people of the city who opposed the brothers' entrance were very surprised at Fadrique, "and told him that because of him, great harm would come to the city . . ." (71). The second item is that while Enrique and Fadrique rested in their lodgings, their companies robbed an isolated Jewish quarter and killed up to 1,200 persons, men and women, young and old. By the end of the chapter, the count's men were knocking down the walls of the main Jewish quarter and entering it through great gaps in the walls. Although the actions of Enrique, Fadrique, and their troops are clearly condemned, it seems that the author is careful to try not to blame Enrique directly. The townspeople criticize only Fadrique. In regard to the action by their troops, it hardly seems likely that the two commanders would shut themselves up in their lodgings to sleep while their soldiers rampaged through the city and a battle raged with their enemy. In contrast, the description of the arrival of Pedro's troops and their efforts to enter the city is effective and entirely credible. The chronicler reports that Pedro arrived very early in the morning on

Monday, 8 May. The river was very low at that time and he had forded it near a village called Pertusa. He had been notified that, if he approached on the side of the city near Saint Martin's bridge, those in the Jewish quarter could let him in. The king ordered some of his troops to attack the bridge and set fire to the gates. Ayala continues: "Some of his men then began to pass over the dams that were in front of the Jewish quarter, for they were drier than they had been in twenty years, and this was in the month of May, as we have said. About three hundred men-at-arms crossed over. The Jews who were in the Jewish quarter helped them and gave them hemp ropes. And they crossed the river over the dams, holding onto the ropes" (72).

In the third chapter, the attention shifts back to the king's half-brothers and their attempts to defend the bridge. The anonymous, marauding troops who attacked the Jewish quarter are replaced by specific knights, under the command of Enrique and Fadrique, who do their best to prevent Pedro's men from crossing the bridge. The statement that the bridge tower had no parapets or battlements to shield the knights, who were all wounded by arrows, is repeated twice in order to give more emphasis to their valiant efforts. The brothers and their supporters agreed that they were in great danger as the number of the king's men who were in the city increased. They also realized that when the king himself entered, all the people would go over to his side. Preferring to die in the field rather than in the city streets, they left the city by the same bridge they had entered. When they arrived at Saint Martin's bridge, the king and his companies had already entered the city. Those who were with the brothers robbed the king's pack animals and supplies. Then, at sunset, they all started back to Talavera.

The whole incident lasted only three days: the first day deals with the unsuccessful negotiations between the brothers and the people of Toledo. On the second day, Enrique and Fadrique enter the city and their troops massacre the Jews. The third day describes the king's arrival, his entrance into the city, and the flight of the nobles. The episode is narrated in three chapters, but these do not correspond to the days. The first chapter, which is the same length as the other two combined, focuses on the motives of the brothers and the reasoning of the Toledans. Ayala's exposition of the psychological aspects of the situation is just as well-drawn as the battle details of the second chapter. The chronicler is less successful in his efforts to separate Enrique from the more reproachable acts of his companions. The overall impression of Enrique is unfavorable, especially if one considers the ending of the chapter that precedes this episode, in which the count, because of his great anger, avenges himself on the town of Colmenar, burning it down and killing many of the inhabitants. Although Ayala cannot defend what the nobles did, he does stress the heroism and bravery of the knights at the bridge. He also attempts to justify their departure from the city as a choice of field of combat rather than a flight from direct confrontation. Furthermore, to balance Enrique's actions and to offset their effect, the following chapter deals with the deaths of a number of citizens of Toledo ordered by the king.

Ayala describes a rather elaborate scheme that was conceived in 1378 to try to trick the king of Navarre into entering Logroño where he could be taken prisoner. The purpose was to win the war with Navarre by means of a psychological ruse, rather than by actually fighting it. The king of France had asked Enrique II to go to war against the king of Navarre because the latter had been plotting with the English to take over some French territories. Enrique had also received word from Pero Manrique, one of his highest ranking officials, that the king of Navarre was trying to bribe him into giving up the city of Logroño. For these two reasons, Enrique instructed Pero Manrique to pretend to give up the city in exchange for a certain amount of money. He would then try to trap the Navarrese king inside. The Castilians prepared by having a large number of troops in the city. Furthermore, in a nearby town there were 600 of Enrique's lancers ready to lend assistance. The word was sent out that the lancers were against Manrique, who was supposedly considered a traitor to Castile. Because of the greed of the king of Navarre, Manrique succeeded in luring him as far as the bridge to the city. Ayala deftly reveals the interplay of emotions and suspicions between Manrique and the king of Navarre. Even though he doubted Manrique's sincerity and suspected a ruse, the king allowed his men-at-arms to enter the city. Manrique went out to invite the king to enter the city also. By this time, the king's distrust of Manrique was stronger than his desire for Logroño. He decided that since his men were already within the city, it would soon be apparent if there were a trick involved. Manrique immediately realized that the king had become very suspicious and would not enter the city. At that point the Castilian knight himself began to suspect that he might be the one deceived. He rushed back over the bridge into the city, fearing that the Navarrese king might try to seize him. The failure of Enrique's plot resulted in open warfare between the two kingdoms.

The Growth of Naval Power

In addition to the two major, full-scale battles—of Nájera and Aljubarrota—described in the chronicles, there is preparation for a large naval battle during the Castilian-Aragonese war. The chapters that pertain to these three important events are fascinating because of their content as well as for what the chronicler has chosen to include, his emphases and arrangement of the material, that is, the encounters themselves plus the surrounding or supporting incidents. The narration of the naval episode is presented in a balanced arrangement of its components: the period of preparation; three efforts to confront the enemy fleet, separated by two land excursions; and, finally, three periods of waiting before the enterprise was abandoned. The episode actually began in August 1358. While Pedro and his troops were attacking the Aragonese city of Guardamar, his ships were destroyed by a strong wind. The preparation then was started which eight months later would result in a great fleet to send against the Aragonese. The king sent orders to his shipyards in Seville to build as many galleys as possible, "for the king had a great deal of wood and all things necessary for galleys in Seville" (94). During the following winter, twelve new galleys were built, fifteen others that were in the shipyard were repaired, and many supplies and weapons were made. In addition, owners of all the ships in Galicia, Asturias, Vizcaya, and Guipúzcoa were instructed to be ready to join the fleet. The description of the flotilla of 128 ships that left Seville in April 1359 contains the number and generic name of each of the four different types of ships included, the country of origin (Castile, Portugal, or Granada), the total number of each type of ship, and the names of the Castilian ship captains.[9] In addition, Ayala, who was one of the officers, notes that sailors were in charge of some of the smaller, swifter galleys which the king was able to send to many different locations because of their maneuverability.

The first attempt to make contact with the enemy fleet was made after the Castilians arrived at Cartagena. Seven galleys were sent out in a futile search for some Aragonese ships to capture. The news of the approach of the large Castilian fleet had traveled quickly and all the ships along the coast of Aragon had put into port. The first land interlude is a return to Guardamar, where they took the town and castle and left personnel and supplies. The second effort to confront the Aragonese occurred when the Castilian ships reached Barcelona and found twelve Aragonese galleys in the harbor. Again, preparations by the Aragonese made it impossible to capture the enemy ships. The galleys were drawn up close to the land so that they could be defended by those on shore. The people of Barcelona had also put many anchors in the sea in front of the ships so that if the Castilians approached, they would run into the anchors and damage their hulls. This information was brought to them by a slave who escaped from the city. Thus, they were able to avoid the hazard, for the anchors plus heavy bombardment from the land and the ships made any seizure of vessels impossible.

During the second land excursion, the Castilians laid siege to the town of Ibiza, on the island of the same name. There is little information supplied concerning this effort because attention remains focused on the naval adventure. Pedro knew that the king of Aragon was preparing forty galleys in order to come and fight with him. Therefore, he had left some of his vessels with captains and armed warriors on the coast. The impending battle seems more imminent because of the details supplied by the chronicler. He lists the number of Aragonese ships from each of the seven ports of origin. He then mentions the two Castilian galleys sent to Mallorca and the two sent to Barcelona, which returned with the same news: "the king of Aragon had left Barcelona and had come to the island of Mallorca. And [they learned] that all his forty armed galleys were already with him, and that his intention and desire was to come and fight with the king of Castile" (105). The chapter ends with a statement about how they obtained this news, followed by a restatement of the news itself. In addition to the repeated mention of the forty Aragonese galleys in this chapter, they are also referred to in the first line of the next three chapters. This repetition reinforces and adds to the atmosphere of suspense and anticipation which has been increasing since the first stages of preparation began. It is effective in terms of sustaining interest as well as in reflecting the significance of this naval effort. The potential confrontation was so significant to Pedro and to Castile because "the whole matter of the war would be decided by that battle, where the kings were to be in person" (105).

Since the Castilian fleet had been described earlier, the author now concentrates on the galley to be used by Pedro. It was the largest one in his fleet, and Ayala notes that it was called Uxel. It had been won along with other Moorish galleys during the reign of Alfonso XI. He states, moreover, that the Moors made the galleys so large in order to transport companies from Africa to Gibraltar and Algeciras. A further impression of its size is given by the fact that the galley had three castles and the capacity to carry forty horses. The mention of the commanders of the galley is one of the rare occasions in which Ayala names himself as a participant, serving as captain on the quarterdeck. There are many details describing the arrangement and maneuvers of the Aragonese galleys. Although Ayala uses almost no adjectives, the scene is visually very impressive due to placement and repetition of verbal phrases. For example, at the end of a fairly long description of the order of the Aragonese ships, the author observes: "and all forty galleys were coming under full sail" (105). The Castilian ships were anchored beneath a high cliff and could not be seen from a distance. In the brief passage describing the Aragonese reaction when they suddenly caught sight of the Castilian fleet, the words "they saw" are repeated five times and "they lowered the sails" and "they took up the oars" are reiterated three times. Following the description and ensuing action, Ayala explains the motivation. The Aragonese wanted to be able to control and maneuver their ships in order to get near shore where the companies on land could help them. Since it was evening, the Aragonese ships entered the River Denia "because at night in the sea, the wind and cold generally increased, and they feared that, with that weather, the [lighter] sailing ships could overtake them" (106). The tension dissipates immediately when the Aragonese decide to take shelter for the night instead of staying in the sea to fight. Even though the Castilians stayed, hoping that the opposing fleet would come out to face them, the long-awaited confrontation never took place. In fact, the Aragonese king had stayed behind in Mallorca. Nevertheless, the venture was of considerable importance as a very impressive show of Castilian naval force, and as evidence that Castilian ships were able to operate in the Mediterranean far from their home bases.

The Battle of Nájera

The Battle of Nájera took place on 3 April 1367. It is possible to consider that all the events since the first resistance of the nobles to Pedro I led to this confrontation. Nevertheless, there are two immediate factors that precipitate it. One is Enrique's alliance with France and Aragon and his claim to be king of Castile and Leon. The other is the fact that the weakness of Pedro's position made it necessary for him to flee to Bayonne to seek military support from the Prince of Wales. Enrique crowned himself king in March of 1366, and Pedro left the country the following summer. In the last two chapters of

1366, Ayala discusses the agreements made between Pedro and the English prince. Although the actual battle scene is narrated in chapter 12 of 1367, the preceding eleven chapters all deal with matters that are part of the war and lead up to the battle. Chapters 1 through 3 focus on events that are serious setbacks to Enrique's battle strategy. In quick succession, the king of Navarre breaks his agreement to deny passage through his country to Pedro and his allies; the Englishman Hugh Calveley and 400 cavalry leave because they cannot fight against their lord, the Prince of Wales; and 600 of Enrique's cavalry desert and go over to Pedro's side. Late in February, Pedro and his allies cross the frontier at Roncesvalles, proceed rapidly to Pamplona, and begin their journey through Alava toward Castile. At the end of chapter 3, the focus is on Enrique as the chronicler comments: "and because of all this, the King Don Enrique did not worry about anything else except to spend each day arranging his people for the battle" (160). The names of a number of important knights are also included at this point.

The next three chapters are an interlude that deals with preparations. Chapter 4 is devoted exclusively to a description of how Enrique ordered his forces for the battle, whereas the corresponding plan for the prince's army is detailed in chapter 5. With the battle order set, it appears that they have disposed of all the preliminaries. However, chapter 6 is concerned with a decision on whether or not Enrique should fight the English. In spite of French advice to the contrary, Enrique's council says they must fight or the Castilians who now support Enrique will go back over to Pedro's side. Near the end of the chapter, the line of action is resumed with a reference to Pedro and his allies advancing through Alava. The chapter closes with Enrique installed in the strong castle of Zaldiaran, with Pedro and the English prepared to fight on the plain below. The three brief chapters that follow contain preconfrontation events that favor Enrique. With unusual restraint, Enrique holds his unassailable position at Zaldiaran. Some of his men are able to capture a number of the enemy while the latter are foraging for food. In addition, an important English knight is killed in a skirmish and others are killed or captured. Again Pedro and his allies prepare for battle, thinking that Enrique's main army is coming. It soon becomes apparent that they can neither bypass Enrique nor fight against him except at great disadvantage. They decide to go back through Alava to Logroño so that Enrique will either have to fight or allow them to enter Castile freely.

At the beginning of chapter 10, Enrique goes to Nájera and is prepared to cut off the enemy's advance at the Najerilla River. With the opposing forces a short distance away at Navarrete, the battle is ready to begin. A last minute exchange of letters between the Prince of Wales and Enrique once more raises a slight possibility of avoiding the conflict. The prince's letter is quoted in chapter 10 and Enrique's response in chapter 11. The two letters are approximately the same length and include their respective justification for their actions. Chapter 11 ends with the prince's reply "that these reasons were not sufficient in order for the battle to be avoided, but that all this was up to the will of God as his mercy would decide, and that there was no other recourse than to resolve it by battle then" (164). The first line of chapter 12 refers back to the location of Enrique's forces as explained at the beginning of chapter 10, once again picking up the temporarily interrupted line of activity. Rather than maintaining his position with the river between him and his opposition, Enrique decides to cross the river and fight in a large open area on the other side. Ayala intrudes into the narration to express the reaction to this plan as well as to explain Enrique's motives: "And many of those who were with him regretted this, for first they had their camp at greater advantage than it was situated afterwards; but the King Don Enrique was a man of great courage and of great vigor. And he said that by all means he wanted to fight in a level place without any advantage" (164). This unwise decision plus the desertion of a number of cavalrymen before the battle, recalling the events at the start of the year, produce a sense of foreboding and seem to prefigure Enrique's defeat.

"And then they moved against each other . . ." (164). With these words, the chronicler begins a vivid eyewitness account of the battle in which he took part as standard bearer for Enrique II. The first to join the battle were the members of the vanguard of each army. After reporting the identifying insignias borne by the knights of the opposing groups, Ayala records details of the pitched battle: "And they went against each other so vigorously that the lances of those on the one side and of those on the other fell to the ground. And they joined together in hand to hand combat. And then they began to wound with swords, battle axes and daggers, those on the side of the King Don Pedro and the Prince of Wales shouting out, using his name, *Guiana, Saint George,* and those on the side of the King Don Enrique, *Castile, Santiago*" (164). When the opposing vanguard fell back a little, Enrique's men believed they were winning and advanced, fighting fiercely.

In the meantime, Don Tello at the head of the cavalry on the left "did not move to fight." When he and his companions saw the enemy approaching, "they did not wait for them, and they left the field, fleeing at breakneck speed" (164). Since there were no cavalry to combat in either of Enrique's wings, the opposing troops attacked the rear of Enrique's vanguard "so that then all those who were on foot in the King Don Enrique's vanguard were dead or captured, for no one helped them, and on all sides they were surrounded by enemies" (164). Although Ayala never states what happened to him personally during the battle, the dreadful helplessness of this statement gives it a poignantly affective quality. He does mention Enrique's banner four times and includes his own name in the list of those who are captured at the end of the battle. In the aftermath of the battle, the exemplary conduct of two French captives is the subject of chapters 13 and 18 (see the discussion above about chivalry at the Battle of Nájera). The four intervening chapters relate the activities of Enrique, Tello, and the kings of Navarre and Aragon immediately after the battle. Finally, there are three chapters that deal with postbattle negotiations between Pedro and the Prince of Wales. Although the battle of Nájera ended in a resounding defeat for Enrique II and his French battle companions, it did not determine the outcome of the war. The chapters that follow the battle narrative itself indicate a lack of resolution and emphasize the grave problems still existing in Castile.

Aljubarrota

The Battle of Aljubarrota, on the other hand, is the definitive event in the Castilian-Portuguese war. The Castilian defeat assured Portuguese independence and firmly established João I as the head of a new Portuguese dynasty. Efforts by Juan I to exert Castilian hegemony over Portugal had dominated his country's policies for several years. His marriage to Beatriz, heir to the Portuguese throne, and the death of Fernando of Portugal shortly thereafter in 1383, seemed to offer a clear path to this objective. Nevertheless, Ayala presents the whole enterprise as an inexorable march toward disaster. Failure of judgment by the king and lack of discipline among the troops had caused Enrique's defeat at Nájera. Juan's eagerness to end Portuguese independence and exert Castilian control led him into the same fatal errors. A series of ill-advised and at times hasty decisions preceded Aljubarrota. When the Portuguese resisted his efforts to take over the throne after the death of Fernando, Juan's council advised consideration and restraint. Instead, Juan reacted by invading the neighboring country in December of 1383. In 1384, the massive siege of Lisbon failed mainly because of devastating illness among the Castilian army. Juan insisted on continuing the costly action and, in consequence, lost a large part of his men and especially his most experienced military leaders. At the beginning of the fateful year of 1385, Juan's total effort was concentrated on building an enormous army to crush opposition in Portugal once and for all. The Portuguese resistance consolidated around the master of Avis, who succeeded in getting himself elected king of Portugal. It is somewhat ironic that the former master of Avis, now João I, claimed his right to the crown by free choice of the people, as Enrique II had done in his usurpation of the Castilian throne. To add to the incongruity, the English, who had opposed Enrique and rejected his reasoning, decided to support the new Portuguese monarch. The news of the election of João I as king of Portugal is reported in chapter 6 of year 1385. This begins the circle of events that have as their center the Battle of Aljubarrota.

As the Portuguese king devoted himself to winning back most of the northern cities between the Miño and Douro rivers, Juan I was planning a two-pronged assault on Portugal. Chapter 8 begins with a summary of the preparations that had already been made for the war. The remainder of the chapter deals with the battle at Troncoso, which is similar to that of Aljubarrota in several respects. A group of Castilian knights with a small army precipitously entered Portugal, near Ciudad Rodrigo, before the archbishop of Toledo could arrive with the rest of the troops. The Portuguese learned of their approach, chose a site, and prepared for battle. When the Castilians saw the Portuguese troops arranged in battle formation, they were divided in their opinion of what they should do. One group favored continuing on their route. If the Portuguese wanted to fight, they would come out of their position and then the Castilians would be glad to face them. Another group insisted "that it would be very shameful for them to see the enemy clearly and not go to fight with them; and that those who heard of it in Castile would misunderstand" (BAE, 98). Unfortunately, pride and concern for fame prevailed over reason.

The Castilians dismounted and began to cross a plowed field while the Portuguese quietly waited. With the heat and dust, by the time the Castilians reached their foes they were in a state of disorderly confusion. Just as they had left Castile before the preparations were completed, their lack of foresight again put them in a dangerous position on the battlefield. Ayala's concern for order and proper battle discipline is emphasized as he uses three synonymous verbs in a row to convey the idea: "desordenaronse, a fueron mal reglados, e non ayuntados como debian" ("they were disordered, badly arranged and not organized as they should have been," [BAE, 99]). The Castilians committed another tactical error when their horsemen got behind the Portuguese and attacked the foot soldiers, preventing them from fleeing. Ayala contrasts the disorderly Castilians with the Portuguese, who stayed calmly in their advantageous position and waited for their enemy to arrive. The Portuguese completely routed the Castilians, wounding one of the captains and killing the other two, as well as most of the Castilian men-at-arms. In the last line of the chapter, Ayala sums up the final effect by noting that from this battle and from their other successes the Portuguese gained more vigor and pride. It is natural to assume that just the opposite effect took place among the Castilians, who could poorly stand to lose additional experienced soldiers. The loss also meant that only a single thrust into Portugal would be possible.

The Battle of Aljubarrota, narrated in chapter 14, parallels that of Troncoso in many ways. The Castilians arrived, with only part of their forces, to find the Portuguese awaiting them in battle formation in a very favorable defensive position. Once again the Castilians disagreed among themselves about their course of action. The discussion prior to the Battle of Troncoso was very brief. In contrast, the opposing arguments before the Battle of Aljubarrota are dealt with at great length, whereas the description of the battle itself is quite abbreviated. There are three fairly long chapters preceding chapter 14 that deal with arguments either encouraging or discouraging the confrontation. In fact, most of the battle chapter is also dedicated to preliminary discussions and plans. Even before Juan I entered Portugal with his army, a dispute arose over whether he should invade or divide his forces into several strong frontier garrisons to fight a war of attrition. The king's spirit was bolstered by the news of a Castilian victory at Mertola. In addition, two other items favored the Castilian position: the seizure of a Portuguese supply convoy and the arrival of the Castilian fleet in Lisbon meant that ample supplies would be available and that Castilian supremacy on the seas was assured. The arguments of those who favored the invasion seem immature and hasty. They insisted that the Portuguese king would not fight, but even if he did, the Castilians were more numerous and much more able. Furthermore, the king should keep his promise to help Santarem and other cities that were still for him. If the king approached, Lisbon would quickly surrender.

Ayala was undoubtedly among those in opposition who presented their view in a long, reasoned argument containing a number of very logical points. The memory of Nájera and the experience gained in the intervening years dampened their zeal for battle. Their objections included the king's illness, the loss of experienced soldiers, the high stakes of the Portuguese and their recent good fortune, the lack of money, and, most important, the vital need for order in a war effort. They urged caution and careful planning in view of the great illness and death that God had sent them during the siege of Lisbon and during the other misfortunes they had undergone. In addition to the typical method of argumentation, Ayala's presence is specifically noted in the last line of their argument: "And they even told the king that if some good arrangement could be made with Portugal, that they would advise him to do it. For they told them, and it was true, that the Master of Avis was willing to make an arrangement and would give him a large part of the kingdom" (BAE, 101).

Although Juan professed agreement with the second group of advisors, his eagerness to invade could not be dampened. Soon after entering Portugal, news arrived that the Portuguese king wanted to fight and was preparing his army for battle. It seemed apparent that he and his advisors wanted to risk all in one big battle. There is a last minute exchange of letters between Juan I and Nuño Alvarez Pereyra, commander of the Portuguese army, but this appears to be no more than a matter of form. The letters are brief and to the point, unlike the longer, more formal letters exchanged between Enrique II and the Prince of Wales before Nájera. Both the Portuguese and the Castilians make impossible demands of each other and end by saying that if the other side insists on a battle, they will leave it up to the will of God, who is surely on their side. Chapter 13 begins with a comment on the Portuguese king's battle arrangements, including a description of the site chosen as well as the number and types of soldiers he had. On the afternoon of the battle, Juan's troops are only a few kilometers away. Ayala gives no details on the size or composition of the Castilian army, probably because it greatly outnumbered that of the opponent. There are a number of delays before the battle begins, but there is no development of an atmosphere of anticipation or suspense before this confrontation. Immediately after commenting about the two armies, Ayala mentions the king's illness which had already lasted two weeks. In addition, the battle chapter begins: "The King Don Juan was lying in the field, propped against a knight, and he was so sick that he could hardly talk" (BAE, 103).

In contrast to the interplay of favorable and unfavorable events that preceded Nájera and served to create a certain tension, the tone here is somber and the outcome seems inevitable. In spite of all the reasons why the battle should be delayed, it is always clear that it will be fought and the Castilians will lose. The chapter in which the battle is described is long, but fully two thirds of it contains arguments against fighting that night. Ayala himself, along with a companion, had visited the Portuguese camp, ostensibly to try to negotiate an agreement. Their real purpose was to observe the enemy's battle arrangements. Although they agreed that a battle was inevitable, they advocated a delay for a number of reasons, which are ably and diplomatically set forth. An elderly, experienced French knight who was there supported their position. He referred to his own battle experiences and stressed the importance of good order and discipline. The views of these three men are similar in tone and content to the reasoning advocated by those who opposed the king's entrance into Portugal in chapter 11. In the same way, those who favored the invasion now urge an immediate attack. Their arguments are emotional and without any basis in logic or experience, resembling those who wanted to attack at Troncoso. The king was genuinely convinced by the more restrained reasoning of the first group and ordered that their counsel be followed. Prior to the battle, Ayala repeats three times that if the vanguard moved forward to fight, it would be impossible for the wings to help, because of the valleys which would be in front of them. In spite of all this, the chronicler reports that:

Some of the king's knights, who were young men and had never been in another battle, were not convinced by that advice, saying that it was cowardice, and, having little respect for the enemy, they began to attack them. And thus it was, as some had feared, that the two wings of the king's battle formation could not fight, for each one of them ran into a valley that they could not cross. And the king's vanguard fought without help from his wings. And in the two wings of the enemy, there were many foot soldiers, and they had many stones and a great many crossbows, and they did a great deal of damage to those in the king's vanguard. Consequently, the vanguard and the two wings of the enemy fought with the king's vanguard alone, for his two wings could not help, nor did they fight. (BAE, 104)

To make matters worse, part of Juan's cavalry repeated the same error they had made at Troncoso and attacked the enemy's rear, forcing the foot soldiers to stand and fight instead of fleeing. With the weary voice of experience, but intent on stressing his message, Ayala continues: "And this is contrary to the good arrangement that the ancients ordered observed in battles, for a man should never put any resistance at the enemy's rear, in order to give him room to flee. And the battle thus begun, those in the vanguard of Portugal had a great advantage, for all of them, with the help of the foot soldiers that they had in their wings, fought with the vanguard of Castile alone, and those of the two wings of Castile did not fight, for they could not cross the valleys that they had in front, as we have said" (BAE, 104). At the beginning of the battle, the king was so weak and sick that his men carried him onto the battlefield on a stretcher. When they noticed that the battle was not going well, they put him on a donkey in case a bit more speed might be needed. When they saw their own people retreating, and some even galloping off the field, they put the king on a horse and quickly got him away from there. The battle narration and the chapter end with the king's escape from the field. In the last line of the chapter, the chronicler notes that the battle lasted barely one-half hour.

The remaining chapters contained in this year are also connected in some way to the disastrous battle. Chapters 15 and 20 deal with the aftermath of the battle in terms of immediate as well as long-term effects. Chapters 17 and 19, like chapter 6, report on more successful efforts by João I to take back Portuguese cities. Chapter 18 contains the report of yet another battle the Castilians lost, although they could have and should have won it. The problem this time was less lack of discipline than lack of spirit. Ayala attributes the defeat mainly to bad luck and concludes: "And this was a great misfortune among all the others that happened in this war after it was begun" (BAE, 106). This battle is cited as another example in a long series of defeats and humiliations suffered by the Castilians in the war against Portugal. The Battle of Aljubarrota decided the outcome and had far-reaching repercussions. Its importance is reflected in the chronicle by its central position in the narrative of year 1385. All the other events from chapter 6 through chapter 20 are important primarily because of their relation to Aljubarrota. The battle descriptions in chapters 8 and 18 in particular have an echolike quality, which reflects, reinforces, and in some ways completes the narration of the main confrontation. The description of the Battle of Aljubarrota in itself is not as interesting or impressive as the Battle of Nájera or even some of the more minor engagements described in the chronicle of Pedro I. Nevertheless, the skillful arrangement of all the contributing elements results in a unified whole that is outstanding in preparation, balance, and total impression.

Chapter Four

Literary Devices in the Chronicles

The Chronicler's Audience

The chronicles of Pero López de Ayala are primarily works of history, but they are a great deal more than an enumeration of dates and incidents. Although the chronicler recognizes the importance of an accurate record of historical events, the value of this record goes beyond the mere accumulation of knowledge. For Ayala, the purpose of knowing about events in the past is that they may serve as a guide for present actions. This is clearly stated in the author's preface and is evident throughout the chronicles, as we have observed in the previous chapter. An occurrence has little significance in itself; it must be seen and understood within a larger context, within a providential scheme of things. Ayala, as a historian with a moral-didactic purpose, is aware of his audience, who will learn from his report and from his interpretation of history. The chronicler's audience was composed primarily of the king, his advisors, and other members of the nobility. Alan Deyermond writes of cultural expansion in the fourteenth and fifteenth centuries and refers to the public to whom were directed increasing numbers of complex prose and poetic compositions.[1] This public included those who were able to read as well as a cultured group to whom works were read.

There is evidence to indicate that Ayala had both of these groups in mind. Just as Kinkade surmised that the poems from the *Rimado de Palacio* were probably read aloud to the monks in the monastery of San Miguel del Monte, we can suggest a similar, but secular, use for the chronicles.[2] There are indications in the works that a great deal of reading aloud went on at the royal court. There are numerous reports of envoys who are sent with messages or letters that they present orally as well as in writing. The letter from the counselor of the Sultan of Babilonia to Juan I contains this statement: "And we read the afore-mentioned letters of the king before his honored ears, and the matter was recounted in the highest councils . . ." (BAE, 82). Throughout the chronicles, there is an impressive number of verbs of saying, including such words as *say, tell, order, beg, advise, counsel, hear, cry,* and *rumor.* Ayala is intent on reporting what people say in addition to what they do. Often this is reported in an indirect, third-person narrative. However, it is not uncommon for the narration to include quotations of the actual words or Ayala's re-creation of them. Some of the techniques used by the chronicler are similar to formulaic devices noted in works of oral composition and transmission. Phrases like "now we will tell," "as we have said," and "as you will hear" occur with fair frequency. It may be acknowledged that the purpose of these phrases is often to facilitate reading. Nevertheless, it is possible that they were also used to assist the hearer in addition to the reader. They serve a variety of functions within the narrative: (1) to refer to something that will be told later (after mentioning the children of María de Padilla)—"about whom we will speak in their place" (123); (2) to return to what was said previously—"As we have told above, the King Don Pedro at the beginning of this year left Seville . . ." (116); (3) to repeat an item of information— "and those of the two wings of Castile did not fight, for they could not pass the valleys that they had in front; as we have said" (BAE, 104); (4) for transition—"Now we will turn to tell about a talk that was held between the kings of Aragon and Navarre after the death of the Infante Don Ferrando" (138); "Thus these things happened as you have heard . . ." (173); "Now the history stops talking about the Count Don Enrique and Don Juan Alfonso and will turn to tell what the King Don Pedro did" (55).

In another instance, two or more functions are combined in order to make sure that everyone knows what the story is about, what was told before and where it is going: "Now we want to turn to tell what the King Don Pedro did after he left Castile, and as we have told that the king of England and the Prince of Wales, his son, were helping the King Don Pedro, now we will tell how the King Don Pedro arrived in Bayonne and what happened. And thus it was that the King Don Pedro arrived at the city of Bayonne . . ." (156). On occasion, the author addresses his audience more personally by including the indirect object pronoun "you," for example, "Now we want to tell you some things that happened in the king's house at this time" (75) and, "As we have said, Don Ferrando de Castro, who was on the King Don Pedro's side, had come to Zamora, but we want to tell you how Zamora had declared in favor of the King Don Enrique . . ." (156).

At other times, he uses an expression like "as we have said" in an oral context, for example, it is included within the quotation of what the counselors of Juan I said to him. Ayala specifically refers to the most important member of his listening public in the chronicle of Juan I. The first reason put forth in opposition to the king's plan to abdicate begins: "First, Sir, you know from chronicles and books about events in Spain that are in your chamber, and they read them to you when it pleases Your Majesty . . ." (BAE, 126).

How to Interest an Audience: The Use of Direct Address

Having his listener or reader in mind, the chronicler uses a variety of means within his narrative to ensure an attentive and interested audience. In addition to aspects already noted, such as descriptive realism, portrayal of motives and strategy, and deft arrangement of elements to form an organic unity, Ayala includes in his chronicles dialogues and one-liners, dramatic scenes, discourses, letters, exempla, prophecies, dreams, sayings, proverbs, and literary portraits. There are a number of narrative passages in the chronicles, particularly in that of Pedro I, that are enlivened and made more impressive by the use of brief quotations, ranging in length from a few words to a line or two. Many of these passages deal with events that are of a dramatic nature. For example, when Enrique II decided to begin using the title of king of Castile and Leon, the nobles who favored him went through the streets of Calahorra shouting "*Real,* for the King Don Enrique!" (148). In identical fashion, after the death of King Fernando of Portugal, some nobles rode down the Rua Nova in Lisbon declaring: "*Real, real* for the Queen Doña Beatriz!" (BAE, 86). Battle cries are another short exclamation, as in the Battle of Nájera, the men on one side shouted "Guiana! Saint George!" and those on the other "Castilla! Santiago!" (164).

Sometimes just a sentence is quoted to emphasize an important point or often to express fear or urgency. When the people of Toro saw Fadrique cross the river to join King Pedro, they were frightened and a great shout went through the village: "We are dead, for the master of Santiago has gone over to the king, and we are left helpless" (80). The feeling of danger involved in Enrique's escape after the Battle of Nájera is heightened when, after the collapse of his horse, one of his men on a swift Moorish charger approaches and says: "Sir, take this horse for yours is not able to move" (166). The gallantry and self-sacrifice implied by this act reflect favorably on the knight as well as on the master who inspired it. After the same battle, Enrique's wife, Juana, managed to escape with the children to the questionable safety of the Aragonese court. Their perilous position is expressed in a less direct way but in words appropriate to the more formal speech of a member of the higher nobility. The uncle of the king of Aragon addresses her: "Madam, I was raised in the chambers of the kings, and I am familiar with and know well the ways of their courts, and I can not say more; but my advice is that you leave here soon and go to France where the King Don Enrique, your husband, is and don't stay in this kingdom of Aragon" (179–80). A line of direct address is used effectively on another occasion when, shortly after the death of Alfonso XI, Leonor de Guzmán realizes that she will no longer have the support of Alfonso Ferrández Coronel. The latter does not want to risk angering Pedro I by helping the former mistress of the dead king, Pedro's father. He therefore tells her that he can no longer continue directing and protecting her lands and properties in Medina Sidonia. Leonor answers, "My dear friend, in truth you are leaving me and my town at a very difficult time, for I don't know now who will want to protect it for me" (16). Leonor's fear and anguish produce a much more intense effect upon listening to the revelation of her emotions in her own words.

Dramatic Scenes

In the farewell scene between Leonor de Guzmán and her son Fadrique, the author effectively portrays the pathos of the situation and the sadness and stoic resignation of the pair. The scene is described simply but with great emotional effect. "And Doña Leonor took the master, her son, and embraced him and kissed him, and was crying with him for a whole hour, and he never again saw Doña Leonor, his mother, after that day, nor did she see him" (22). The effectiveness of this passage is heightened through contrast with the brief chapters that precede and follow it. The previous chapter describes a meeting between the king and Fadrique in which the latter treats the king with great courtesy. Pedro in turn reaffirms Fadrique's authority as master of Santiago. In the chapter following Leonor's death, there seems to be the possibility of a violent confrontation when the king seeks out another of Leonor's sons, Tello, and asks him if he knows about his mother's death. Tello, perhaps through fear of the king, simply responds: "Sir, I have no other father or mother except your majesty" (23). With the exception of Tello's response, there are no direct quotes in these chapters, although they have a marked dramatic quality.

One of the most vivid and highly charged scenes in the chronicle of Pedro I describes the assassination of the knights who accompany the Queen Mother María at Toro and her reaction to their deaths. The first part of the episode is slow paced and very effective visually. After stating that "the queen came out *(salió),*" all the verbs are in the imperfect tense or are present participles. The names of the four knights who accompany her are listed, and the names of the two who hold her by the arm are repeated. One of the latter, Ruy González, had agreed to convince the queen to leave the palace, in exchange for a letter of pardon from King Pedro. As the small group advances, Ruy González carries the letter high over his head, calling out that, by virtue of the king's letter, his safety is assured. Pedro, however, replies that the time period has expired and the letter is no longer valid.

The group's arrival at a small bridge in front of the palace cuts off the possibility of retreat and signals an acceleration of the action. The focus swiftly moves from one individual to another, describing the killing of the two knights on either side of the queen in graphic detail, including the name of the squire who does the killing, the weapons used, and the sites of the wounds. The death of the other two knights is stated but not described. The brutality of the event overwhelms the queen who "fell to the ground senseless, as if she were dead . . ." (81). The final portion of this episode sustains the strong visual impact. As the queen recovers consciousness, she sees her knights around her, dead and stripped of their clothing. She begins "to shout loudly, cursing the king her son, saying that he had dishonored her and wounded her forever, and that she would rather die than live . . ." (81). While she is shouting, the king simply has her lifted up and carried off to the palace. The large number of twinning words or doublets throughout the episode echo and magnify the visual and dramatic effect. Some examples include two women (the queen and Doña Juana), two masters of Calatrava, two squires, and two killings. This is further intensified in the final scene by several pairs of words: "dead and stripped," "cursing and saying," "had dishonored her and had wounded her," "to die rather than live," and "lifted up and carried away" ("muertos e desnudos, maldiziendo e diziendo, la desonrrara e la lastimara, más quería morir que bevir," and "levantar e leuar"). It is appropriate that

this scene be described in such a vivid fashion, as it represents the end
of Queen Mother María's power. She is given permission to go to live
with her father, King Alfonso, in Portugal where she dies the following
year. This episode also can be considered the definitive turning point
for Pedro, who thereafter seems obsessed with the punishment of the
rebels.

The Departure from Burgos

A well-constructed episode, which uses direct address in combination
with a number of other recourses, deals with the departure of Pedro
I from Burgos in 1366. Within this chronicle, the failure of the king
to make a stand against Enrique in defense of the city of Burgos is
viewed as the final justification for many nobles to switch loyalties.
Although Ayala accompanied Pedro to the south, it may be that it
was important to him to explain his subsequent change of allegiance.
The incident occurs soon after Enrique declared himself king in Calahorra.
The chapter begins with a summary of the news about Enrique, which
reached Pedro in Burgos. The last line of the brief report states that
Pedro reacted with great fear and suspicion. After the summary statement,
the basic components of the episode itself are: the opening frame
sentence, the confrontation between Pedro and the people of Burgos,
the meeting between Pedro and the knight in charge of the castle, an
act of vengeance ordered by the king, and the closing frame sentence.
The frame sentence at the beginning supplies specific information and
reveals the cause of the conflict: "And one day, Saturday, the day
before Palm Sunday, in the morning, without saying anything to the
gentlemen and knights that were with him, he mounted up in order
to leave and abandon the city of Burgos" (148). Beginning with this
action by Pedro, the focus alternates between the king and the people.
The narrative continues with the people's reaction: "And those of the
city, when they found out about it, came to him to his palace, the
most important and best people of the city, and told him and begged
him and asked him, please, that he not leave and abandon them this
way . . ." (148). In terms of the total length of the episode, the
confrontation with the people is most extensive, and the quoted conversation between the citizens and the king is located at the center of
the entire incident.

In preparation for the scene using direct address, the arguments of
both sides are presented. The use of alternation between the king and

the citizens reinforces the contrast presented in their arguments.[3] It is obvious that there are two opposite perceptions and assessments of the situation. The people are willing to sacrifice everything in order to defend the city. Even the king's response stresses the qualities of the people, that is, dependability and loyalty. The king's reply and the people's second statement are each divided in two parts, further underlining the comparison. The first half of the citizens' statement is further subdivided and a number of negatives are used. The people again begged "that he not leave the city *and* that he not believe in any way such news as they were telling him / *but* rather he should be certain that . . . [the count's] intention was to come to Burgos" (148; my italics). The author begins the first dialogue at the point when the people decide that it is useless to try to convince the king any more. Their words form a succinct analysis of the situation: "Sir, since Your Grace knows that your enemies are eight leagues from here, and you do not want to wait for them here *in this your very noble city of Burgos* with so many good companies as you have here, what do you order us to do and how can we defend ourselves?" (148–49; my italics). As mentioned above, this segment is placed at the center of the episode and the phrase "in this your very noble city of Burgos" is at the exact center of the Spanish quotation according to the syllable count. The brevity and abruptness of Pedro's reply reflects his haste to leave. He answers: "I order you to do the best you can" (149). The people continue to insist on a more explicit reply from the king and repeat their question: " 'What do you want us to do? And therefore, Sir, God forbid, if the case is such that we can not defend ourselves, do you remove the pledge and oath of homage that for this city we have made once and twice and three times?' And the king said: 'Yes' " (149).

In addition to the general structure or arrangement of events and the effective use of direct discourse, other literary devices the author employs in this episode are alternation, contrast, parallelism, and repetition. Reiteration of both words and concepts, as well as the use of synonymous expressions, stress the most important points. Terms referring to *leaving* occur fifteen times, using four different verbs; the verb *defend,* seven times, and *asking*—in the context of the people's efforts to get the king to stay—twelve times, also involving four different verbs. Moreover, "the city of Burgos" or "the city" is mentioned a total of fifteen times, plus the central reference with multiple modifiers that occurs in the dialogue. There are also many other, less extensive examples of repetition, for example, the fact that Enrique is eight leagues away is stated twice, as is the people's desire that a written record be made of their request and of the king's reply.

Another reinforcing technique is references to silence, all referring to the king. At the beginning of the episode the chronicler states that Pedro was leaving "without saying a word," in the middle "he did not want to hear them," and at the end "The king did not answer him." The meeting between Pedro and Ruy Pérez, the knight in charge of the castle, echoes the confrontation with the citizens and also reinforces the idea of abandonment. Ruy Pérez asks the king what he wants him to do about the castle, since the king is leaving the city and the knight cannot defend it. In response to the king's order to defend the castle, Ruy Pérez says: "Sir, I do not have power to defend it, since you are leaving your city of Burgos" (149). This line receives additional emphasis by being the only part of this segment that is put in the form of a quotation. Before leaving the city, Pedro orders the death of a man who had helped Enrique. This act of vengeance is included by the author as a characterizing device. The closing frame sentence ends the episode by repeating part of the opening, reporting the departure and adding the date: "And the King Don Pedro left the city of Burgos Saturday, the day before Palm Sunday, which was the 28th day of March of this same year" (149).

Individual Death Scenes

Among the many episodes of dramatic quality, three that relate individual death scenes are of outstanding literary merit. These deal with the killing of Garci Laso, Alfonso Ferrández Coronel, and Fadrique, a half-brother of Pedro I. All of these scenes are included in the chronicle of Pedro I, although Juan Alfonso de Alburquerque, and not the king, is responsible for the first two deaths. The chapter telling how Garci Laso died begins with Pedro's arrival in Burgos on a certain Saturday. What the members of his council tell the king, plus the chronicler's explanation, forms the background for what is about to happen. Ayala's interest in motivation is apparent as approximately one fourth of the chapter is devoted to the narrative explaining the reasons for Alburquerque's hatred of Garci Laso. This portion ends with a summary statement. Reference back to the words which opened the chapter, "And then that day Saturday at night . . ." (24), signals the end of the background and the beginning of the main action. The queen mother's message to Garci Laso, warning him not to go to the palace the next day under any circumstances, indicates what will probably happen to him and creates a mood of apprehension.

Five sections of narrative alternate with four of direct discourse. The first narrative section describes Garci Laso's arrival at the palace. Three elements add to the tense atmosphere: the doors to the palace are heavily guarded, the queen mother and the bishop of Palencia leave as soon as Garci Laso enters the king's chambers, and the three men of Burgos who accompany him are seized and taken away. In the first dramatized segment, there is a progression from the very vague to the very precise. Juan Alfonso is the first to speak: " '*Alcalde,* you know what you have to do.' And the *alcalde* then approached the king and said to him quietly, with Don Juan Alfonso hearing it: 'Sir, you order this, for I would not say it.' And then the king said in a very low voice, but so that those who were there would hear it: 'Bowmen, seize Garci Laso' " (24). The narrative then names three of Juan Alfonso's men and the weapons they had. A reference back to the king's order to seize Garci Laso bridges the interruption and leads to the next portion of the dramatization and the following narrative, both of which focus on Garci Laso. The petition of the condemned man reveals his resignation regarding his physical danger and the concern for his spiritual well-being that he experiences. Juan Alfonso's manipulation of the young king is apparent as he again speaks to Pedro: "Sir, order what is to be done" (24). The astute advisor never directly orders the soldiers to act, but by prompting the king, he achieves his goal.

The tension is increased by another delay in the next narrative. Pedro orders the guards to tell the bowmen to kill Garci Laso. The incredulous bowmen do not dare to carry out the order without hearing it from the king himself. Their doubts are emphasized as one of them asks the king: "Sir, what do you order done to Garci Laso?" and the king replies: "I order you to kill him" (24). This dialogue parallels the first one in form and content, moving the action to its climax. The killing and the following events are described in vivid detail: "And then the bowman entered and hit him in the head with a bludgeon. And Iohan Ferrández Chamorro wounded him with a dagger and stabbed him with many wounds until he died. And the king ordered that they throw him in the street, and thus it was done" (24). As he did in the chapter dealing with the departure from Burgos, Ayala follows his practice of signaling the beginning and ending of the incident by referring to the date. In this case, he adds that since the king had just arrived in the city, the bulls were running in the plaza and trampling the body. Also, later that week, as the king was eating, the three men who had been arrested the day Garci Laso was seized were taken past the royal lodgings on their way to be killed. These added details further intensify the effect of the passage.

The chapter dealing with Garci Laso is characterized by an atmosphere of tension created by uncertainty, hesitation, and delays. By isolating the intervening narrative material, most of which serves to augment the suspense or to take the place of stage direction, the dialogues can be joined to produce a single dramatized scene. On the other hand, in the chapter concerning Alfonso Ferrández Coronel, there is no suspense created. Even his death is not narrated in any detail. In fact, Alfonso Ferrández's awareness of the inevitability of his death is an important factor in the portrayal of his character. The chapter can be divided into nine segments. The first one relates the situation. The city of Aguilar had already been under siege for four months, and the description of the final assault provides an interesting picture of one phase of medieval warfare (see chapter 3). The last section of the episode reports the king's arrival and the deaths of Alfonso Ferrández and five others. It concludes: "And the king ordered the walls of Aguilar torn down" (38), thus ending the battle for possession of the city. Segments 3, 5, and 7 are narratives in which a change of location takes place and the action is advanced. The remaining four parts, that is, 2, 4, 6, and 8, are dialogues that alternate with the narrative passages. In each dialogue Alfonso Ferrández converses with a different person. These passages serve primarily for characterization of Alfonso and contain some of the most memorable lines in the chronicles (see the discussion of Ferrández Coronel as a chivalric example in chapter 3). Three of the dialogues contain questions about the motives for his actions. To the last query, he answers: "Don Iohan Alfonso, this is Castile that makes men and breaks them, I understood it well, but it was not my good fortune to turn away from this evil . . ." (37).

Fratricide: The Death of Fadrique

The account of the assassination of Fadrique, illegitimate half-brother of Pedro I and twin of Enrique II, is one of the few portions of the chronicles that has been the object of any critical attention in terms of its literary value. In his brief remarks about this episode, the Italian critic Alberto Várvaro speaks of "a refined ability of a narrator who develops his tale subtly calculating all its effects."[4] Fadrique's death is part of Pedro's campaign to eliminate all those who had been involved in his imprisonment at Toro. Although the event itself is narrated in chapter 3 of year 1358, the surrounding chapters are important to the total effect. Chapter 2 is devoted to part of Pedro's preparation for Fadrique's arrival in Seville. The chapter begins with a clear and concise statement of the situation: "The King Don Pedro, being in Seville, knew that the master of Santiago, Don Fadrique his brother, was coming, for he had sent for him, and he had planned to kill him" (90). A manipulating, perfidious, scheming Pedro is the center of attention throughout the chapter. The action takes place in the king's chambers the morning of Fadrique's arrival. In the first paragraph, Ayala describes the meeting between Pedro, the Infante Juan of Aragon, and Diego Pérez Sarmiento. Unbeknown to the infante, Diego Pérez was really guarding him, according to the king's orders. The meeting begins with an atmosphere of intrigue as Pedro has the other two men swear oaths of secrecy on a cross and on the gospels. The remainder of the chapter achieves a strong sense of actuality by being entirely in dialogue, with the exception of lines to point out the speaker and two sentences that indicate Pedro's emotions. Pedro's revelation of his plan to kill his half-brothers Fadrique and Tello and give Vizcaya to the infante has even better results than he had hoped. The infante feels honored to be privy to the king's secret, approves the plan, and volunteers to kill Fadrique himself. However, part of Pedro's plan is spoiled when Diego Pérez advises the infante not to do it, saying that there is no scarcity of soldiers to do the killing. The king, who had been so pleased with the success of his bait, now is upset, and never liked Diego Pérez from then on, because he really wanted the infante to kill Fadrique.

The next chapter opens with the same words as chapter 2: "The King Don Pedro being in Seville," but now the focus is on Fadrique, who is the subject of the first sentence. The character and motives of Pedro, established so well in the previous chapter, contrast with those of Fadrique. Ayala portrays the rebellious half-brother as an ideal vassal, characterized by obedience, service, and respect. Fadrique, master of Santiago, had just come from capturing the city of Jumilla, which he did, according to the narrator, "to do service to the king, for the Master Don Fadrique wanted to serve the king and to please him" (90). The author adds two more phrases, "he went to pay reverence to the king" and "he kissed his hand," in order to reinforce this impression. Although the reader knows Pedro's plan, the king's cordial reception and solicitous inquiries about Fadrique's lodgings seem to be a warm brotherly reception. When Pedro sends Fadrique to arrange his quarters, Ayala explains the king's real motive—to get rid of the men accompanying his brother. Fadrique goes from the king's chambers to those of María de Padilla in order to greet her and her children. Through her reaction and by praising her, the author expresses disapproval of Pedro's actions: "And Doña María knew all that was planned against the master, and when she saw him, she had such a sad look that everyone would be able to understand it, for she was a good woman and of good sense, and she did not approve of the things the king was doing. And she was very grieved by the death that was ordered for the master" (90). In spite of her apparently obvious show of emotion, Fadrique does not yet notice that something is amiss.

The action, from Fadrique's arrival at the palace to his eventual murder, proceeds in a very measured and detailed fashion. The chapter itself is one of the longer ones in the chronicle, covering nearly two folios as compared with the previous chapter whose length is one-half folio. The scenes follow one another almost in slow motion until the actual attack on Fadrique, which occurs well past the middle of the chapter. Each succeeding stage brings Fadrique closer to his death and increases the anticipatory tension. Fadrique himself seems unaware of what is happening long after many others have become alarmed. From María's chambers, he returns to the courtyard where he discovers that all his animals are gone. Ayala again intervenes to tell why this was done. Throughout, an exquisite dramatic irony is created by the audience's complete awareness of the reality of the situation, in contrast to the lack of knowledge on the part of the participants. The author reports that Fadrique "did not know if he should go back to the king or what he should do" (90). One of Fadrique's men realizes that something bad is happening. His brief warning to Fadrique is put in direct address, lending a greater sense of urgency to his words. The author adds that he said it many times. He then explains the man's reasoning—that Fadrique might escape, or at least they could not kill him without many others dying first. While this is going on, two brothers, who "did not know anything about this," arrive with a simple, but chilling, message from the king: "Sir, the king calls you" (91).

The scenes that follow doubtlessly represent the height of dramatism in Ayala's work. At this moment, Fadrique begins to be aware of his situation but seems to be inexorably swept along by it. "And the master turned to go to the king, frightened, for he feared something bad. And thus as he went entering through the doors of the palaces and the chambers, he was going more and more without company, for those who had the doors under guard, thus had ordered the doorkeepers not to allow them in" (91). Fadrique, master of Santiago, arrived near where the king was, now only accompanied by two knights and the master of Calatrava Diego García, "who did not know about this matter." The repeated mention of doors continues. The emphasis had been on Fadrique's passing through them and becoming increasingly isolated as he neared the king. In the sentence which describes their arrival at the king's palace, the *door* is mentioned four times, but now it is locked. Two brief dialogues, carried on through a small wicket in the door, are inserted at this point. They contribute to the vividness of the scene, but at the same time serve to prolong the final moment of suspense before the action resumes.

In the first dialogue, a delay is caused by the ambiguity of the king's order to "arrest the master," since both the Master of Santiago and of Calatrava were there. The bowman has to ask: "Which one of them, Sir, will I arrest?" The king replies: "The master of Santiago" (91). In spite of the fact that the four-line dialogue delays the action, tension is increased by the use of very brief lines, commands, and repetition of the verb *arrest* or *seize*. Fadrique seems stunned: "And the master was silent, very frightened." The voice of the king is heard again: "Bowmen, kill the master of Santiago" (91). Although the command is explicit, there is another pause because the bowmen do not realize who is giving the order and therefore do not dare to attack the king's brother. One of the men in the king's chamber shouts loudly: "Traitors, what are you doing? Don't you see that the king orders you to kill the master?" These questions stress the king's responsibility for the deed. They also further deepen the ironic effect by calling the soldiers traitors when the king is the one committing the traitorous act.

The narration continues: "And the bowmen, when they saw that the king was ordering it, began to raise their maces to wound the Master Don Fadrique." The action is interrupted, with their arms raised in the air, in order to give the names of the soldiers. In this split second, Fadrique wrenches free from his captor, leaps into the corral, and puts his hand to his sword. The futility of his effort to defend himself is emphasized by stating that he never succeeded in drawing his sword, describing in detail the problem with the sword and finally repeating that he was not able to unsheath it. Again the soldiers approach to wound him, but they can not because Fadrique darts so swiftly from one spot to another. Although the attack on Fadrique is described in detail, this is not the final climax of the action which, after a brief narrative interlude, continues to build. The focus is now on the king who looks for others to kill. All of Fadrique's men had fled or hidden, except for Sancho Ruiz de Villegas.

The site of the action now returns to María de Padilla's chambers, where Sancho Ruiz takes refuge and tries to avoid death by holding the king's daughter Beatriz. Pedro snatches the child from Sancho Ruiz's arms and, there in the presence of the women and children, stabs him with a dagger he had in his belt. The frantic pace continues as the king returns to the courtyard where he discovers that Fadrique is still not dead. Pedro again takes the dagger from his belt, presumably stained with the blood of his recent victim, and has one of his men kill Fadrique with it. The real climax to this violent episode lies in the matter-of-fact statement which ends it on a particularly horrifying note: "And after this was done, the king sat down to eat where the master was lying dead in a corral . . ." (91). Before the chapter ends, the plot line is picked up involving the king's promise to give Vizcaya to the Infante Juan of Aragon. Also, in order to further emphasize the bloodshed caused by Pedro, the chronicler reports a series of orders sent out by the king to have persons killed all over the country. The word *kill* is repeated seven times in the last few lines of the chapter.

The chapters that follow continue to amplify the overall impression. Chapter 4 describes the king's unsuccessful pursuit of another brother, Tello, to Vizcaya. Chapter 5 deals with the Infante Juan's efforts to get the king to keep his promise to give him Vizcaya. The fairly lengthy exposition of this problem can be explained by two reasons. First, throughout the chronicles, Ayala tends to devote more time and space to those things that he considers most important to the kingdom, such as the schism, Aljubarrota, problems and wars with royal relatives, and negotiations with the duke of Lancaster to settle the dynastic problems. In addition, however, he also consistently includes things that are personally important to him, especially those that affect his property and his home area of Alava, for example, discussion of *behetrías*, borders with Navarre, disputes with clergy over who has the right to collect tithes, and anything else involving the seigniory of Vizcaya. In this case, the episode explains the origin of the kings themselves being lord of Vizcaya. Second, it has been repeatedly implied that the king would betray the infante, but Pedro's secret meeting with the Basque knights makes it explicit. Ironically, it also recalls the secret plotting between the king and the infante in chapter 2.

Chapter 6 completes the cycle of events begun in chapter 2. It contains a short, violent, and gory description of the death of the infante. The directness of the episode forms an effective contrast with the carefully developed suspense of chapter 3. In response to the king's summons, the infante arrives at the palace. "And a soldier of the king, called Juan Diente, hit the infante in the head with a mace. And other soldiers with maces came and wounded him. And the infante, wounded as he was, still had not fallen on the ground, and went, completely unconscious, toward where Juan Ferrández de Henestrosa, chief valet of the king, was in the chamber. And Juan Ferrández, when he saw him coming, took out a sword that he had and put it in front of him, saying: 'Get back! Get back!' And a soldier of the king, called Gonçalo Rezio, hit the infante in the head with a mace, and then he fell dead on the ground" (93). The chapter continues with a brief paragraph in which the narrator adds that the king had the body thrown out of the window onto the plaza and later cast into the river at Burgos. The last sentence concludes the entire five-chapter sequence. It is typical of the technique Ayala uses to end an episode: "And the Infante Don Juan died Tuesday, the twelfth day of June, two weeks after the Master Don Fadrique died in Seville" (93).

The Schism

The chronicle of Pedro I is so rich in evidence of Ayala's skill and literary creativity that examples from the other chronicles seem to pale by comparison. There are a number of episodes in them, however, in which the chronicler uses similar literary techniques. As in the chronicle of King Pedro, the subject matter is inherently dramatic, generally involving a death or arrest of a high noble.[5] A somewhat different event, but of equal dramatic potential, is the report of the beginning of the schism in the church. Rather than being a dramatic reproduction of an event reported as if by an eyewitness, a message is given to Enrique II by couriers sent from the king of France. The message begins with "he sent them to say that . . . ," and each succeeding clause starts "and that. . . ." This repetition would seem to reduce the sense of immediacy and the dramatic impact but, on the contrary, it is effective in producing the impression of a rapid succession of events. The episode consists of three sections of decreasing length. The first deals with the pressure brought to bear on the cardinals by the people of Rome, the second treats of the election of the two popes, and the third serves as summary and reinforcement.

The first part begins after the death of Pope Gregory when the cardinals, following custom, entered the conclave to elect a new pope. The crowd or mob spirit of the Romans is deftly conveyed: "those of the city of Rome, armed and with great merriment, ringing bells, arrived at the conclave where the cardinals were gathered, and with great shouts they said to them: 'We want a Roman pope, or at least Italian'" (BAE, 35). The atmosphere of celebration suddenly changes to one of violence, as the armed Romans forcibly enter the conclave. Ayala uses two synonymous verbs to describe the breaking of the locks. Also, the people's desire for a Roman pope is repeated in direct address but "we want" is replaced by the command "give us." The intensity of the cardinals' reaction is increased by the mounting up of five expressions referring to their fear and its effect. "And that the cardinals had such great terror, for they thought they would be killed, and they did not know what they were doing; and that then, with great fear, they did not know what to say . . ." (BAE, 35). In order to escape from the Romans, one of the cardinals falsely says that the archbishop of St. Peter is the pope.

The second part dispenses with the repetition of "and that . . ." but uses a series of ten preterite tense verbs to give the impression of rushing about and of precipitous action. This reflects the people's insistence and willingness to accept anyone as long as he is Italian, as well as the cardinals' impulsiveness in the election of Urban VI and their haste to leave Rome. After the cardinals arrived in another city, they elected a different pope. For dramatic impact, the chronicler reports this as if it happened immediately, when in fact it occurred five months later. The final section begins in the same way that the first did—by referring to the message sent by the king of France. Having related the events in parts 1 and 2, part 3 specifically states the conclusion. First, the cardinals claim that the first election was done through coercion and fear. Words referring to fear are used eight times in the narrative. Therefore, they consider the act null and the second election the real and true choice. The last sentence of the chapter finally reveals the French king's purpose: to convince Enrique to support Clement VII as true pope. The content and form are effectively joined and enhanced by the use of direct address, details, and repetition of terms and structures.

Other Uses of Direct Discourse

Two other forms of direct discourse that are used frequently throughout the chronicles are speeches and letters. Just as short exclamations and dialogues occur more frequently in the chronicle of Pedro I, so do short speeches characterized by personal involvement and intensity on the part of the speaker. The two main uses of short speeches are to defend one's own actions or to convince another to do something. Some examples of convincing speeches are the following: the queen mother and Pedro's aunt try to persuade him not to return to María de Padilla (42); after Pedro's imprisonment at Toro, his aunt insists that it is all in his best interests (65); and a relative of Juan Núñez de Prado wants him to fight rather than to surrender to the king (49). These speeches usually have two parts: the first to state the situation or the problem and the second to give advice, reasons, or rationalizations. Self-defense speeches are generally longer and enumerate the accusation and the justifications. For instance, a knight who is not Pedro's vassal explains why he is wearing the insignia of the *Orden de la Banda* (40); Juan Alfonso de Alburquerque pleads his case to the king of Portugal in defense of what he did when he ruled Castile on Pedro's behalf (50–51); Samuel Levi explains his conduct and his plan for solution of money problems (75); and the duke of Benavente talks to Enrique III to defend his rebellious actions (BAE, 225–26).

A number of lengthy discourses are quoted that were presented most often at meetings of the Cortes during the reign of Enrique II and Juan I. These are given in response to decisions by the king or to his request for advice, for example, the nobles' advice to Enrique II regarding distribution of *behetrías* and the council's advice to Juan I concerning Count Alfonso, the invasion of Portugal, and his plan to abdicate. The form of argumentation is similar in each of these speeches. In addition to a clear statement of the problem and an orderly, methodical form of argumentation, Ayala usually includes an appeal to historical precedent to support the proposed solution or to refute the king's plan. Reference is generally made to the desire to serve the king, who is praised for his good intentions and his abilities. The problems are analyzed to consider every possible ramification. The recommendation is stated early in the discussion and repeated again at the end. Ayala was a member of the deliberating bodies, and it is likely that he served as spokesperson for the nobles or the council in the Cortes when these speeches were delivered.

There are a number of speeches that are really the oral delivery of a letter and, as such, their function is the same as that of a letter or of a written response. This type of quotation occurs most frequently in the chronicles of Juan I and Enrique III, where several letters of condolence are included. Written statements occur when Juan I notifies the country of his decision in favor of Pope Clement VII, when the Cortes responds to Enrique III, and when Pope Benedict XIII replies to the French dukes. In the chronicle of Enrique III, two documents are quoted in full, the will of Juan I and the agreement all the cardinals signed before entering the conclave to elect a new pope in 1394. During the reigns of these two kings, Ayala was involved at the highest levels of government and had access to these documents. Sometimes they are quoted simply to supply information regarding important events or decisions. At other times the letters provide variety of form or of language. In the latter case, the pope's letters tend to be couched in formal, elegant language and style, while the letters from the sultan of Babilonia (Juan I, year 5, chapter 3) are flowery and extravagant. In the chronicle of Enrique III, written and oral messages form an important stylistic component used for alternation and interruption.

Novelistic Elements

In the chronicle of King Pedro, there are a few unique examples of the use of fictional elements, probably derived from ballads and folklore. These occur near the end of the chronicle and, for the most part, serve a propagandistic function. In the two letters from the Moor, Ayala uses a novelistic form similar to that of Juan Manuel in the *Conde Lucanor*. Pedro writes letters to a Moor "whom he trusted, and was his friend, and was a great scholar and philosopher and advisor to the king of Granada . . ." (174). The Moor answers giving advice by means of exempla, analogies, proverbs, and sayings. The Moor compares misfortunes, and possibly his advice, to harsh and bitter medicine, which is detested by the patient but holds the only hope for a return to health. The first letter contains the exemplum about the shepherd and the wolf. The good shepherd who protects and cares for his flock is contrasted to the man whose neighbor's lamb was carried off by a wolf. The man followed and rescued the lamb. When his neighbor asked what became of the animal, he replied: "I cut his throat and I ate him." The neighbor disgustedly commented: "You and the wolf are just alike" (175–76).

The Moor's second letter was supposedly found in a chest in Pedro's bedroom. The letter explains that the king had a prophetic message that was "found among the books and prophecies that . . . Merlin composed" (192). According to the prophecy, a huge, ravenous, preying, black bird will be born and will devour everything. In the end, however, the bird will suffer, die, and be eternally condemned. More than half of the letter is dedicated to the Moor's interpretation, in which the bird symbolizes Pedro and his greed. The interpretation serves as a summary of Pedro's crimes and a justification for Enrique's murder of his brother.

Several events that foreshadow Pedro's eventual fate are also reported near the end of the chronicle and have a novelistic tone. Just before the first battle of Nájera against Enrique, a priest requested a private audience with Pedro. The priest said that Saint Dominic had appeared to him in a dream and had instructed him to tell the king: "that you should be certain that if you are not careful, that the Count Don Enrique, your brother, will kill you with his own hands" (114). The king was frightened by this prediction, but because he believed that it was just a plot against him, he had the priest burned to death. The battle took place, but it went so badly for Enrique that the king could have surrounded him and undoubtedly would have killed his half-brother. However, on the road to Nájera, Pedro met one of his men who was loudly lamenting the death of his uncle at the hands of Enrique's men. Pedro took this as a sign that he was not to continue the battle in spite of the urging of his advisors. The chronicler gives the following interpretation: "It was not God's will for him to do it, nor was he pleased with this advice. And this was, as we have said, the will of God that the count was not captured, as it later appeared, that God had plans for him" (114–15).

Pedro received another warning in a letter from Gutier Ferrández de Toledo. Ferrández advised: "And now, Sir, I tell you just at the point of my death, that this will be my last counsel, that if you do not lay up the knife, and stop causing such deaths as these, that you have lost your kingdom, and you yourself are in danger. And I ask you please to refrain, for I speak with you loyally, for in such an hour as this I should only say the truth" (117). The final message was brought to Pedro by a mysterious shepherd shortly before the death of his wife Blanca in 1361. The shepherd said that God had sent him to warn the king that he would be severely punished for any harm done to

Blanca, but if Pedro returned to her, they would have a son to inherit the kingdom.

Literary Portraits

In addition to characterization, motivation, and mental processes that are interwoven with the narrative throughout the chronicles, Ayala excels with his literary portraits. They are more or less clearly defined and separate from the narrative thread and occur generally after a person's death. These portraits are precursors of the type of history in the fifteenth century that highlights biographical data. Ayala includes portraits only of royalty. There is also a brief sketch of María de Padilla, probably included because the children she and Pedro had, who are listed at the end of the portrait, are later incorporated into the royal family. Doña María possesses the desirable characteristics that are generally ascribed to noble women of her time: she is of good lineage, devout, beautiful, small, and intelligent. (See also the portrait of Blanca de Borbón in chapter 3.) She is described several times earlier in the chronicle, always with the same attributes.

The extremely laudatory portrait of Alfonso XI, at the beginning of the chronicle of Pedro I, contrasts with that of Pedro himself at the end of the work. Alfonso is praised above all for his military accomplishments and the honor he brought to Castile. Ayala concludes: "And he was a very great warrior against the Moors and a very noble knight. And King Don Alfonso was not very large physically, but with a good physique and strength. He was fair, blond, forceful and fortunate in wars" (14). Following his characteristic pattern, the chronicler gives the date, place of death, and a description of the person, including physical traits as well as temperament and moral qualities.

Early in Pedro's reign, when he was about to go to war with Aragon, Ayala describes the king by stressing only character traits and pointing out the influence his advisors had over him: "And the king did it just as they advised him, for the king was a young man at the age of twenty-three years. And he was a man of great courage and boisterous, and he always loved wars . . ." (p. 83). The final portraits of Pedro, Enrique II, and Juan I are preceded by detailed and dramatic descriptions of their deaths. Both Pedro and Juan met violent ends. Enrique II is the only one to die peacefully in bed, an ironic twist in view of the way he came to the throne and how he lived. The scene during his last hours is impressive, however, due to the pomp and ceremony involved and the description of his rich garments of gold, fur, and precious stones. The circumstances of Juan I's accidental death are described in detail. Ayala then mentions the tragic fate that seemed to haunt the young king throughout his reign: "The King Don Juan was of good manners and good customs and without any anger in spite of the fact that he always had very little luck in all his affairs . . ." (BAE, 143). The portrait continues with the date of birth, age, length of reign, and description of the king.

The circumstances surrounding Pedro's death, which are apparently based on the true event, seem as fantastic as any invention. In dramatism and suspense, it rivals any other event in the chronicles and contains the literary devices that Ayala is accustomed to use in such scenes, such as direct discourse, staccato commands, silences, and so on. The narration of the confrontation between the two brothers differs from the chronicler's usual style of writing in one respect. Instead of continuing his practice of reporting as if he were present, he states that others say that certain words and actions took place. The episode culminates this way: "And the King Don Enrique still doubted if it was he. And they say that the King Don Pedro said: "Yo so. Yo so" ("It is I. It is I"). And then the King Don Enrique recognized him, and wounded him with a dagger in the face. And they say that both of them, the King Don Pedro and the King Don Enrique, fell on the ground. And being on the ground, the King Don Enrique wounded him with other wounds" (198).

The portrait of Pedro ends the chronicle of his reign. After a lengthy enumeration of dates—Pedro's birth, ascension to the throne, and death, including mention of his age three times—Ayala begins the description of the king: "And King Don Pedro was quite large physically, fair, blond and he lisped a little. And he was a good hunter of birds and a very hard worker. And he was very temperate and moderate in eating and drinking. And he slept little and loved women a great deal. He was very industrious in war and he was very covetous of gathering treasure and jewels" (198). Up to this point, the author seems to present Pedro as a composite of good and bad traits. He proceeds, however, to give evidence of his greed by a lengthy enumeration of the jewels, gold, silver, and money that were inventoried in various royal treasuries. Moreover, Ayala condemns Pedro for killing many people, thereby bringing great evil on the kingdom. There is the implication of an almost mystical or preordained completion of a circle with the repetition of "March," referring to the date of Alfonso XI's death, March 1350; the occasion when Enrique crowned himself king in Calahorra, March 1366; and finally the death of Pedro, March 1369.

Chapter Five

Ayala's Impartiality, Humanism, and Minor Works

The Chronicles: The Problem of Impartiality

The chronicles of Pero López de Ayala, particularly that of Pedro I, have provoked admiration, interest, and controversy among readers and critics during most of the six centuries since they were written. This has occurred for a number of reasons. First, the change of dynasty by violent overthrow of the legitimate monarch made some justification necessary. Ayala's first version of Pedro's reign, that is, the one found in the manuscripts of the *Abreviada* tradition, contains the report of a number of episodes that condemn Pedro I by emphasizing the cruel and irrational nature of the king and his actions. The simple recourse of condemnation of Pedro and exaltation of Enrique II is complicated, however, by the reconciliation of the two dynastic lines, with the marriage of the grandchildren of the two contenders. Consequently, we find some of the harshest and most condemnatory passages omitted from the *Vulgar* version.

Another reason lies in the person of Pedro I himself and the events that occurred during his reign. The paradoxical and powerful figure of the king dominates the scene for most of the two decades of his reign. The principal source for knowledge of events in this period is, of course, the chronicle of Ayala. The chronicler's impartiality, and at times even his veracity, has been questioned because he reports so many barbarous acts, and because he views Pedro I primarily as a negative example. Ayala's support of the Trastamaran pretender and his later involvement in the royal court further clouds the picture. The literary nature of these narratives and our chronicler's acute awareness of literary style must also be taken into account.

The assessment of Ayala's reliability has generally been based on which of the contrasting portrayals of King Pedro is accepted: a cruel and degenerate murderer or a virtuous dispenser of justice. The Catholic kings were especially interested in defending their ancestor. The sixteenth and seventeenth centuries saw some extreme examples of apologies for Pedro and attacks on Ayala as well as equally extreme defenders of the opposite view.[1] The sixteenth-century Aragonese historian Gerónimo Zurita accepts Ayala as a reliable source and includes little moralizing about Pedro's acts. Later, critics like Menéndez y Pelayo, Fueter, and Sánchez Alonso were enthusiastic in their defense of Ayala.[2] Other recent critics such as Lapesa and Tate observe that there was a conflict between Pedro and Ayala because the latter was a member of the nobility and, moreover, was a moralist.

Let us consider how Ayala would have written the chronicle of this turbulent period if he had remained among the few Petrine loyalists. Certainly the events themselves would have to stay the same but a change in the emphasis or manner of narration would be essential. In addition, the fictional portion would not be included, that is, the Moor's letters and the segments originating in popular romances and dealing with the mysterious appearances of shepherds and priests. More importantly, the author's moral and philosophical stance would have to be completely reversed. Although some view Ayala as a self-serving turncoat whose writing smacks of political propaganda, this judgment, like all other critical opinions, is based on the reader's interpretation of the author's intention.[3] In the absence of convincing extratextual evidence, it seems correct to attribute Ayala's criticism of Pedro's conduct to the historian's teleological concept of nature and to his loyalty to his country, demonstrated throughout decades of service.[4] Ayala could not condone the cruelties and injustices of Pedro. Indeed, he no doubt emphasized them while minimizing the undesirable acts of his successors. Nevertheless, his change of allegiance did not prevent him from criticizing other kings when their conduct merited censure nor from including crimes and treacherous acts that were committed by the king's enemies as well as those by the king himself. Ayala's concept of the plan of history may also have guided his choice of ballad material. For example, he does not include those containing slanderous accusations that Pedro was illegitimate. Instead, he chooses the ones that contain prophetic material.

Throughout the chronicle of Pedro and perhaps to a somewhat lesser degree in the other three chronicles, Ayala seems conscious of the narrative techniques that can best suit both his stylistic and political objectives. Ironically, in his attempt to dramatize the rise and fall of Pedro I, Ayala has succeeded in reshaping historical writing into a literary form similar in some ways to classical tragedy. Pedro first lives as a tragically flawed king in Ayala's chronicle and later has mythical and legendary development in the *romances* and *comedias* of Spain's Golden Age. To what extent Ayala shapes historical facts for political, moral, or literary reasons may never be known completely. Although Ayala probably reviewed his personal notes and chancery documents, it is doubtful that these sources contained the dramatic dialogue, the detailed and graphic descriptions, and the other literary devices found in the chronicles.

Ayala as a Humanist

Another controversy that persists is whether one can justifiably classify Ayala as a humanist, that is, whether the chronicler makes a clean break with the spirit and culture of the Middle Ages. In the nineteenth century Menéndez y Pelayo affirmed that Ayala was the initiator and exponent of an intellectual movement. There are many critics who still in the twentieth century allude to the humanism of the chronicler although too often in vague or abstract terms. Valbuena Prat, Américo Castro, Sánchez Alonso, and others refer to a new direction or perspective evidenced in the Ayala chronicles.[5] Valbuena Prat elaborates on his concept of Ayala, the modern man: "In fact, his skillful position before morality and history, his concept of the world, his attraction for the classical and ethical themes reveal the paradoxical synthesis of the Renaissance man, from Boccaccio to Maquiavelli." Lapesa believes that the Ayala chronicles are characterized by a new orientation without ridding themselves of the ideological and artistic influence of the medieval tradition. Also he says: "With Chancellor Ayala medieval Spanish literature ends and humanism begins to appear."[6] Angel del Río, speaking of the chronicles, points to the biographical style and the dramatization of events and personages as indexes of the transition of the medieval tradition and the entry of humanist or pre-Renaissance characteristics.[7]

It is tempting to give a strong endorsement of these views, especially since they contain so many valid observations concerning Ayala's chronicles. Especially perceptive are those that place the chancellor on the frontier between the medieval and pre-Renaissance worlds. Not only does he continue to employ devices and commonplaces from the medieval tradition, but his interest in the classics, and particularly his translation of Livy's *Decades,* fail to result in close imitation or unmistakable resonances of the classics in Ayala's writing.[8] The longer speeches, as well as the letters, rarely reflect closely any personal aspect of the speaker's character. Nevertheless, these communications do vary stylistically from one speaker to another. For example in the *Chronicle of Juan I,* the letter from the Oriental potentate, the sultan of Babilonia, is the most elaborately ornamented in content and structure. The pope's letter to Enrique III, following the death of the latter's father, is characterized by a loftiness of tone and sentiment befitting the leader of the Catholic church addressing one of his favorite sons. In fact, in almost all instances, it is clearly apparent when Ayala himself is the speaker. Although he is not usually named, his speeches are characterized by their rational approach and clear, methodical organization. In addition to changes in the speeches according to the speaker, their placement in context is worthy of note. Although a similar observation can be made of all four chronicles, the best example of speeches and letters being used for variation of content and style occurs in the *Chronicle of Enrique III.*

One aspect that sets the Italian humanists apart from their predecessors is the literary characteristics contained in their histories. It must be admitted that Ayala's conscious narrative art and technique places him on the side of these historians. Like his Italian counterparts, Ayala goes to great pains to portray the thought processes and motives that underlie the actions of such figures as Pedro I, Enrique II, Leonor de Guzmán, the archbishop of Toledo Pedro Tenorio, and many others. These portrayals are frequently found couched in skillfully created dramatic scenes. It is this aspect, especially in the *Chronicle of Pedro I,* that has received the greatest critical attention and most consistent praise.[9] A note of caution is in order at this point, however. The difference between Ayala and the humanists lies primarily in their concept of history. The Italian humanists view history as a record of human actions *inspired by human motives.* Their emphasis is on the individual personality, and their most important concern is with the fortunes of great, even bigger than life persons. In this respect, Ayala goes a different route, remaining firmly within the medieval mold with his emphasis on a providential framework and the exemplary function of historiography. Although, properly speaking, Ayala cannot be considered a fourteenth-century Spanish humanist, his chronicles at least indicate the beginning of the change from the medieval period toward humanism and the later Renaissance.

Minor Works: Translations

Fernán Pérez de Guzmán, Ayala's nephew, recognizes the chancellor's importance as a translator and lists some of his works: "Because of him some books are known in Castile which were unknown before: such as that of Titus Livy, the most notable Roman history; the *Fall of Princes;* the *Morals* of Saint Gregory; Isidore, *De summo bono;* that of Boethius; the *Historia de Troya.*"[10] Other works attributed to Ayala are the *Family Tree of the Ayala Line, The Book of Job,* and the *Flowers of the Morals of Job.* Ayala translated Livy's *Decades* based primarily on the French version of Pierre Berçuire rather than the original Latin text.[11] In the prologue to the *Decades,* Menéndez y Pelayo also attests to Ayala's contribution to learning in fourteenth-century Castile, observing that "the books that constituted the common and basic core of the erudition of medieval times passed through the hands of the Chancellor."[12] Undoubtedly, Ayala was motivated by national pride and a desire to enhance his country's culture by translating important foreign works into Castilian. He was an avid reader and was particularly fond of the classics. For example, Ayala emphasizes the nature of Livy's work and lists the benefits to be gained from reading it. He recommends the work to princes and nobles as a manual of military tactics and as a source of moral and political inspiration. Also, Ayala mentions the Goths as exemplary ancestors of the Castilian kings and recalls the names and deeds of those kings who preceded Enrique III. In his analysis of the *Decades* the chancellor points out two chivalric virtues that are desirable for honor and glory—order and discipline. This recalls Ayala's emphasis on these attributes in his chronicles, especially when dealing with the Battle of Aljubarrota.

Livy himself believed that history, having a moral purpose, was a guide to life. Further, the historian was obligated to report truthfully, to build and develop the historical narrative, and to embellish it in a literary style. Curt Wittlin emphasizes the importance given to this translation by historians and philologists "in the development of the Castilian language and prose, in the humanistic background of the translator and of his generation, and in the influence that he had on the beginnings of the Castilian Renaissance."[13] Another work translated by Ayala which also deals with morals is the *De summo bono* of Isidore of Seville. The work presents a broad spectrum of thoughts about the Christian life, including serious and scholarly ideas on theology along with more subjective considerations of social behavior. The translation of the first eight books of Boccaccio's *De casibus virorum illustrium* (The fall of princes) has also been attributed to Ayala.[14] Lapesa notes that Boccaccio's work renewed the pagan view of fortune personified as being restless and fickle. He further observes that this idea of fortune was "present, by action or reaction, in all of the literatures of the same century." Ayala's translation of Boethius's *De consolatione* became one of the favorite readings of fifteenth-century Spain. Kinkade observes that Ayala's translations and commentary on the works of Isidore of Seville, Boethius, and Saint Gregory "reveal his inclination, if in a lesser degree, toward the type of exegesis which Saint Jerome favored."[15]

In addition to that section of the *Rimado* which comprises the poetic version of the *Morals* of Saint Gregory and the Book of Job, Ayala has been credited with the translation of these works as well as a collection of sayings and proverbs translated from the *Morals* and entitled *The Flowers of the Morals of Job*. The *Morals* is a long treatise written by Saint Gregory on the Book of Job. A further discussion of the Book of Job and associated works is found in the chapter on the *Rimado*.

The Book of Falconry

The *Libro de la caza de las aves* (Book of Falconry), according to its prologue, was written by Pero López de Ayala during his imprisonment in Portugal, 1385–88. The prologue contains other pertinent information, including the dedication of the work to Don Gonzalo de Mena, bishop of Burgos. Ayala states that the memory of the bishop and their friendship consoled him during his captivity, explaining that "if a friend is beset with troubles, true friendship offers consolation and great relief in the midst of sadness and adversity."[16] Recalling happier times, the author praises the bishop's skill in falconry and says that the bishop was his inspiration for writing this work. Also, Ayala gives the purpose of the work—to teach and to entertain—which he discusses at some length. For example, the reader is reminded that men should avoid idleness, which only nurtures evil, and "by consequence thoughts are nurtured in one's heart and from them result sadness and mortification" (53). In addition to the harm that may come to the soul, the body can be vulnerable and therefore one must exercise to keep in shape and to build up resistance against fatigue and disease. An ideal type of exercise is falconry, which is described as follows: "it was necessary that there be persons who were skilled in the art of capturing valiant birds, domesticating and taming them, making them good friends of man; and afterwards, with these same birds, one could catch other birds that flew bravely and proudly in the air" (54).

Ayala's book on falconry is evidence of the continued interest among the aristocracy in an ancient sport that was practiced in Asia several centuries before the Christian era and much later was brought to northern Europe by the Germanic tribes and to southern Europe by the Arabs. During the Middle Ages, the privileged classes, comprising royalty and nobility, were enthusiastic about falconry, a sport or form of entertainment enjoyed by both men and women. Don Juan Manuel, in his book about hunting, notes that a nobleman who went hunting would take along at least fifteen birds of different species as well as a retinue of handlers and helpers. Among the upper classes, a falcon was a highly valued gift. In Spain, falcons were imported from distant places— Norway, Iceland, England, Germany, or Tunis. Strict rules governed and regulated the sport, and there were precise criteria for classifying and evaluating the birds. The falcons or hawks were classified according to wing formation—pointed or rounded—or according to flight habits— high fliers or low fliers. Among those falcons classified as high fliers are the *nebli* and the *bahari,* which were considered noble birds and whose use was reserved for nobility and royalty. In addition to hiring falconers, many kings and princes raised and trained their birds personally.

In Spain during the Middle Ages from the tenth through the fifteenth centuries, there are many references to falconry in chronicles and in poems, for example, in the *Poema de Mio Cid* where the vacant perches, once filled with falcons, are symbolic of the great loss suffered by the Cid as he prepares to leave Castile and go into exile. Many technical works on the art of falconry appeared during the time of Alfonso X among the Arabs and the Christians.[17] With the invention of firearms and because of the high cost of this sport, interest in falconry waned toward the end of the fifteenth century.

The Art of Bird Handling

The complete title of Ayala's work comprises the topics to be discussed, that is, falconry, the species of falcons, and their diseases and treatment. The prologue contains the table of contents, which lists forty-seven chapter headings including chapter 8—how the *nebli* falcon should be handled and certain training rules; chapter 9—how the falcon should be deloused; chapter 15—about the falcon that has worms; chapter

24—about falcons that are wounded by birds; chapter 40—what you will do after your falcon has moulted; and chapter 45—about the migration of birds. In the last chapter (47), Ayala discusses medical equipment and supplies, and lists more than sixty medicines the falconer should carry with him to treat his birds. After a general listing of the principal birds of prey and five species of falcons, Ayala focuses on the *neblí* falcon, his favorite. The *neblí* species is considered genteel everywhere and "is the lord and prince of the birds of prey" (80) and "is the noblest and the best" of the falcons (62). In subsequent chapters, Ayala describes the other species of falcons and then returns to the *neblí,* using it as a model to discuss the techniques and rules in the handling and training of falcons. Ayala repeatedly insists on gentleness and tender care in handling the birds and stresses a preference for experienced and skilled trainers. The author reminds the distinguished owners of falcons not to forget to give wine to the hardworking trainers and their helpers.

Adaptation of Sources

During the Middle Ages there was little concern for what we would today label plagiarism. Writers often used paragraphs, pages, and even entire chapters from another author's work without acknowledging their sources. Certainly, Ayala, as a borrower, is no exception inasmuch as he translated from Portuguese the *Livro de falcoaría* written by Pero Menino, falconer of King Fernando of Portugal, and placed it in his own work. The borrowed work comprises chapters 11–39 in Ayala's work and appears almost entirely without changes or suppressions. Nevertheless, Ayala does add some material throughout the Menino work to clarify, reinforce, or elaborate on certain points. For example, to Menino's discussion of wounded falcons Ayala adds: "If the wound is small and there is no need to sew it up, wash it with wine and boiled absinth every two days . . . until the wound has a good color" (46). Sometimes Ayala documents the borrowed Menino material, citing someone by name who had been successful in employing a certain technique or cure. In chapter 29—on treating a falcon whose wing is broken—the author concludes with the following observation: "I saw Ruy González de Illescas, King Pedro's falconer, carrying a falcon whose wing had been broken when it swooped down upon a crane. Afterward the bird was cured and later I saw it kill many cranes just as skillfully as it did before" (137).

In the portion of the work that Ayala himself wrote, his style is clear and precise with an apparent affinity for details and clinical observations. The clarity and organization of the work reflect the author's mastery of his subject as well as his expertise as an experienced hunter. Unlike the *Rimado* and the chronicles, Ayala refrains from moralizing and sermonizing in the *Book of Falconry* and, in contrast, concentrates on the didactic, that is, on teaching and informing. Although the work is written for both the beginner and the more experienced hunter, much of the material seems quite basic and practical. In spite of the apparent scientific and objective nature of the topic, Ayala maintains a highly personal tone throughout the work and establishes an informal author-reader relationship by using the familiar form of address. Lapesa refers to Ayala's vivid imagination, which accentuates or enhances the charms of falconry and adds: "Aside from the technical curiosity, the work is of interest because of the delightful lexicon and the meticulous and exact descriptions."[18] In addition to the effective descriptions, Ayala's added documentation, often in the form of short autobiographical anecdotes, lends charm to the technical discussions. Lebrero refers to Ayala's traditional and revolutionary attitude with respect to his didactic purpose and concludes that Ayala makes use of earlier medieval techniques and attempts to create what is necessary for adornment and vitality in his work.

Chapter Six
Rimado de Palacio

Introduction

The *Rimado de Palacio* was completed in 1404, only a few years prior to Ayala's death. This is not to imply, however, that all of the poetry it contains is the product of the author's last years. The work consists of a large number of poems whose composition undoubtedly spans decades and whose impetus springs from the experiences of a long, adventurous life as well as from periods of reading and meditation. Because of the collection's varied content and structure, it defies simple descriptive labels and easy analysis. To say that it is a didactic-moral work or a long confessional poem is true. Nonetheless, this would slight the literary value and variety of Ayala's forcefully sober verse. Furthermore, it would cast into the background Ayala's fine, satirically traced pictures of medieval society that have, above all else, attracted readers to the *Rimado*. These scenes of contemporary society and court life are found in the first part of the book, along with other poems that arise from the chancellor's personal experiences and his reflections. The more extensive final part of the work, an adaptation of the *Morals* of Saint Gregory, provides a somewhat different focus, that of doctrine.[1] Applying this focus to the overall work as shown in the following chart, stanzas 1–919 would pertain to experience and stanzas 920–2168 would represent doctrine.[2]

Topic

	Stanzas
Introduction	1–20
Confession	
The Ten Commandments	21–63
The Seven Deadly Sins	64–127
Charitable Acts	128–51
The Five Senses	152–74
Spiritual Works of Mercy	175–90
The Schism	191–216

The *Rimado* comprises 2,168 stanzas that total more than 8,000 lines. Ayala uses the verse form of *cuaderna vía* for the majority of his stanzas. *Cuaderna vía* is a system of versification characterized by stanzas of four lines, each line having fourteen syllables, with a caesura after the seventh syllable, and consonantal rhyme *(aaaa)*. There is some variety of versification in the *Rimado,* particularly among the lyrical religious poems, which are often written in *arte mayor,* of twelve syllables, and *arte menor,* of seven or eight syllables. The two principal and more complete manuscripts of the *Rimado* are *E* and *N,* both of which date from the fifteenth century. Three other manuscripts are either fragments or very incomplete. Several titles have been assigned to the work including *Libro del Palacio,* which appears in the codex of the Biblioteca Nacional (Madrid), a reference by the Marqués de Santillana to "a book about the ways of the palace," and Fernán Pérez de Guzmán's reference to a "rhymed book." Later, during the modern period, scholars dropped the word "book," made "rhymed" a noun, and began calling the work *Rimado de Palacio,* the title that is still generally accepted today.

Sources for the *Rimado*

One of the difficulties in determining the sources used by Ayala is that one cannot always tell whether the author remembered passages from a work, whether the source was at hand, or whether the author was merely familiar with a work. However, there are some sources that the poet translated closely and others from which he made direct borrowings. It is evident that throughout the *Rimado* Ayala is deeply influenced by the Bible, particularly the Book of Job and other portions of the Old Testament, including the Book of Kings, Psalms, and Isaiah. The second part of the *Rimado* is devoted entirely to a poetic adaptation of the Book of Job from the *Morals* by Saint Gregory.

Various treatises concerning the education and conduct of princes and rulers were well-known to most educated nobles of the time. Ayala's interest and involvement with this topic is not only evident in his chronicles but also in the rather extensive sections of the *Rimado* devoted to advice for governing. Helen Sears notes the likelihood that the chancellor "had read the *De regimine principum* of Egidio Colonna and remembered certain of its illustrations and figures of speech, as well as many of its opinions on the subject of government. . . . That a common body of similes and maxims originating in church literature and the classics may account for certain similarities between the *Flores de filosofía* and the *Rimado* and between the *Castigos e documentos (Advice and Documents)* and the *Rimado.*"[3] Certainly, the materials in the *Rimado* concerning governing are a blend of Ayala's own experiences as a statesman and his knowledge of other works available to him concerning this subject.

Among Castilian sources, there are similarities or references in the *Rimado* that recall passages from the *Libro de buen amor,* particularly some of the descriptions in the lyrical poems dedicated to the Virgin.[4] Also, it is possible that Ayala was familiar with the *Cantigas* of Alfonso el Sabio. Several scholars have noted the similarities of the confessional part of the *Rimado* with a prose work in romance entitled *Libro de la justiçia de la vida espiritual,* which was written toward the end of the fourteenth century. Other prose works that may have been read by Ayala are the *Libro infinido* and the *Libro de los estados* by Don Juan Manuel and the *Libro de los consejeros et de los consejos,* possibly written by Ayala's uncle, Gómez Barroso.

Plan and Content of the *Rimado*

The first part of the *Rimado* is organized around a core of personal experiences, suffering, confession, and repentance. Ayala, the poet, introduces himself as a sinner and promises to make his confession to the best of his ability with God's help. He attributes his inclination to sin frequently to his being made of lowly earth, and therefore he hopes for God's pardon. In the following discussion of the Ten Commandments, the poet defines each of them and indicates in what manner he had sinned to break the commandment. For example, the third commandment was broken because the poet worked his animals and his servants more than he should have and further confesses: "On that day I hunted with birds and dogs, / I gave little thought to doing holy works" (30 cd).

In addition to a definition or discussion of each of the seven deadly sins, Ayala laments having committed each sin and then asks for forgiveness. Continuing with the numerical groupings of sins, or virtues, there follow the Seven Charitable Acts, which include feeding the hungry, clothing the naked, giving drink to the thirsty, and visiting the sick. To demonstrate how he failed to observe the latter charitable act, Ayala confesses that he loathed visiting the sick and that he would vomit whenever he thought about it.

In commenting on the sins committed because of the senses, the poet reveals information about his early contact with literature. The fact that the book was read aloud to him gives further evidence of a listening as well as a reading public, an aspect that Ayala seemed to bear in mind when writing both his poetic and prose works. He confesses that the sense of hearing caused him to sin because of the pleasure he derived from listening to books about dreams and fantasies, adding that he wasted many hours hearing about characters like Amadis and Lançarote.[5] In contrast to the Seven Charitable Acts, the Seven Spiritual Works are not as clearly defined and seem to overlap. For example, the first of these works is to guide or instruct one who is ignorant. Ayala says that one must teach an ignorant person what to do and what to say: "if God gave you brains, you should share them with him [ignorant person] / and you will never regret such an act" (178 cd).

It is generally agreed that the first discussion of the schism in the *Rimado* (191–216) was written soon after the election of Clement VII in September of 1378. The other pope, Urban VI, was elected the previous April. With respect to this grave situation with the church, Ayala professes to be a simple man and of little learning who dares to suggest that the problem of the schism be resolved through deliberations in council. The section on the clergy immediately follows the section on the schism, being of a somewhat similar subject matter. The *Rimado* discusses such topics as the decadence of the clergy and other elements of society in a direct and candid manner. Apparently Ayala had no fear of reprisal for his scathing and mordant satire of the clergy who "don't know how to be moderate in their life-styles, who love the world a great deal and never think about death" (218 cd). From the material and topics of the next section, on governing of the republic, critics have suggested that Ayala satirizes the reign of Pedro I and suggest the date of composition in the 1360s.[6] The prayer that follows the short section on the cardinal virtues forms an important part of the confessional of the poet. In addition to his petitions for mercy and forgiveness from God, Ayala also discourses on the value of prayer which among other blessings is beneficial because it causes one's anger toward another to dissipate and one is pardoned, just as God pardoned the Jews for His suffering and death.

Because of the general nature of the *Rimado*, the almost total absence of humor does not come as a surprise. However, there are several examples of the comic or tragicomic in the section on events in the palace. For example, Ayala presents a short narrative concerning the problems of a former court favorite who had left the court to serve his king in war. On his return, the courtier is subjected to humiliating and frustrating treatment, especially from the doorkeepers. There are several comic scenes in which the court favorite has to treat the doorkeepers with deference for fear of being thrown out of the castle. Not only do the court favorites have problems, but so do the kings, who often before they come of age are victimized by the nobles and knights. In the section entitled "Advice for Everybody," the poet meditates on a variety of themes or topics, including life, death, the transitory nature of worldly treasures, the virtue of inner peace, and divine judgment. The following section, entitled "Advice for the Governing of the Republic," is narrower in its range of application. In addition to kings, advice is also given to judges, advisors to kings, and ambassadors.

The last section in the first part of the *Rimado* comprises the *Cancionero,* a collection of thirteen poems dedicated to God or to the Virgin Mary, plus sixty-seven stanzas dealing with the topic of the schism. The latter section is placed after the seventh devotional poem. Some of the poems to the Virgin are promises made by the poet to go on a pilgrimage to worship her in specific shrines or cathedrals—Monserrat, Toledo, and Guadalupe. The poem "Non entres en juicio" (Don't condemn) resembles a summary of the confession of the past in the beginning sections of the work. All of the commandments and works of charity along with the different sins are recalled by the poet: "Of all my sins I make confession, / And You, by your grace, make me contrite" (743 ab). In the last part of the *Rimado,* the poet has glossed the *Morals* of Saint Gregory the Great and the Book of Job. Whereas the first part of the *Rimado* seems based on the life of the poet, that is, more autobiographical, this second part reflects the poet's preoccupation and reflection on doctrine. Ayala seeks to offer guidance and consolation to others, who like himself have many problems and tribulations. Also, he attempts to define the Christian roles of the rulers and the ruled.

Themes: Traditional

Although Ayala drew on his own life and experiences, the themes or topics of the *Rimado* still fall within the medieval and orthodox tradition. While there is considerable variety and overlapping in the topics included, they can nevertheless be grouped into several general categories: social, personal or confessional, and doctrinal. Because of Ayala's concern for the schism and his preoccupation with life and death, these topics will be discussed as separate items. With the possible exception of the satire, the themes are presented and developed in a direct and serious manner. The predominant verse form of *cuaderna vía*, with its characteristic mono-rhyme and uniform syllabication, seems most compatible to the sobriety and explicitness of such themes as death, original sin, war, and justice. Some of the themes are associated with well-known commonplaces that have appeared in other works of *cuaderna vía*.

Social Themes

The development of social themes in the *Rimado* is accomplished primarily through the use of satire. On following Ayala's presentation of the different professional or vocational groups and the various levels of society satirized in the work, one has the distinct impression of previewing the picaresque almost two centuries in advance. Among the several groups satirized is the clergy, who are depicted with unrelenting censure by the poet as shameful servants of the church who have no pangs of conscience and who are prone to forget the Holy Scripture. Many of these false clerics bribe and pay for their ordination and are thus able to pass their examinations miraculously without any difficulty. The poet is appalled at the manner in which some clerics handle the Holy Eucharist: "they take it in their hands without any love for God / without being confessed yet and, what is worse,/ they have another grief with them each night" (221 bcd). The "grief" is a veiled reference to the clerics' concubines.

Another group that falls under the poet's ax is the merchant class whose representatives lie, perjure, and "forget about God and their souls; they never think about dying" (298 d). An especially apt humorous

description is the picture of the merchants' stores which were always
kept dark so that the customers could not see exactly what they were
buying. On the other hand, when it was time for the customer to pay,
the merchants would throw open all the doors and windows in order
to count their money. Similar to the merchants' motivation is that of
the lawyers, described in the *Rimado* as avaricious and ever watchful
to seize the opportunity to cheat their clients. Ayala narrates the case
of a client who ends up poverty stricken after giving all of his money
and possessions to a lawyer who prolongs the lawsuit and eventually
loses the case. As a final gesture, the lawyer suggests that the client
appeal the verdict, accepting as payment the man's last possessions—
his mule and his scarf. The gullible client believes that his verdict will
be reversed in twenty days. Of course, now that the client has nothing
left to give, he waits in vain to hear from the lawyer who disappears
and never returns. Some of the more biting satire is directed against
the Jews, who are portrayed in the traditional medieval mold as
avaricious, scheming, and heartless, particularly in their jobs as tax
collectors and in the stereotyped profession of moneylenders.

Ayala does not overlook even the kings and princes whose motives
and actions are too often suspect. Just as clerical censure was directed
to the individual clergyman and not to the universal church, the criticism
of kings refers to the monarch as an individual and does not censure
or attack the monarchy as an institution. Much of the satire directed
to persons in the royal courts would fall in the category of social and
political. The section entitled "Events in the Palace" clearly reflects the
poet's real experiences and observations during the reigns of four kings,
a period covering more than a half century. As noted earlier, Ayala
makes use of many narrative anecdotes or exempla to develop his ideas
concerning the difficult problems of kings and the rise and fall of court
favorites. From the descriptions of kings hounded by petitioners, robbed
by the nobles, and beset with internal problems of government as well
as threats of war from other countries, he may well have wondered
how so many could envy or covet such high station in life. The fact
that periods of peace were almost unknown to Ayala in his long lifetime
may partially explain his longing for this ideal state. He affirms that
peace is wonderful, that it is good for the people and drives away
bitter thoughts that attempt to dominate one's heart. Moreover, the
wise king is one who will strive to rule with peace and not war, and
"the king who loves peace will have many subjects in his kingdom"
(529 ab). It follows that whereas peace implies happiness, prosperity,

and harmony, all is lost with war. Also, the poet insists that above all, the people love and trust a king who fights to maintain peace.

Personal/Confessional Topics

In addition to the general format of the confessional section mentioned earlier, throughout the confession Ayala inserts items that are autobiographically significant. Although one may question the constant insistence on his modesty, humility, and even mediocre intelligence and ability, Ayala's confession is not merely a literary exercise, but rather a sincere self-criticism, and to a great extent it represents real and experienced sinning by the poet. When Ayala pleads, "I weep about it [dishonoring and mistreating his parents], because I am so guilty: / I entreat you for mercy, Lord, / let me be forgiven" (34 cd), it is hardly likely that he is impervious to real suffering and repentance. In one passage, Ayala confesses that he loved beautiful clothes and yet he was not always willing to help clothe the poor. He laments the fact that many needy persons may have died because of the cold weather. As a concluding thought to this transgression, the poet reminds us that God is the ultimate judge and he is just in administering retributive punishment. The poet's confession that he could have had a condemned man saved from prison is a most convincing autobiographical fact when one remembers that Ayala enjoyed many privileges and great power in his important posts. Reference is frequently made by the poet to his imprisonment and suffering, both physical and spiritual. One of the transitional stanzas in Ayala's *Cancionero* reflects his personal anguish and suffering: "I can't prolong my sermon anymore, / because I am troubled in body and in spirit / and very much angered with this prison of mine, / and I would like to turn my heart to God" (729). In the poems dedicated to the Virgin there are strong reminders of the *Cantigas* of Alfonso el Sabio and possibly some of the *Milagros* of Berceo. However, as Lapesa notes, "the tormented tone and the heated immediacy of the circumstances distinguish them notably from the Alfonsine cantigas. . . ."[8] Typical descriptions of the poet's imprisonment include being left in a dark prison, lying suffering and afflicted in irons and chains, and being shut up in a shadowy and dark jail. Since Ayala suffered two periods of imprisonment after Nájera and Aljubarrota, it is necessary to interpret these references as more than traditional allusions to the prison of the corruptible flesh. They must, at least in part, reflect his own experiences.

Doctrine

At first glance one is tempted to consider the first part of the *Rimado* as a section that does not belong, because of being very different in theme from the second part, which comprises almost two thirds of the entire work. Nevertheless, Ayala's glosses, that is, his metrical commentary on the *Morals* of Saint Gregory and the Book of Job, are an attempt to provide guidance and encouragement to persons who are heir to the eternal problem of unmerited suffering. The material dealing with Job echoes and reinforces the personal or confessional tone of the poet, who must recognize and submit to the divine will of God. Ayala imitates Job who, in spite of his complaints to the Lord about his situation, is commonly considered the paragon of patience and obedience. He refers to his tribulations, such as his imprisonment, which test his faith and piety. Also, in a political sense, the glosses offer advice to rulers and their subjects, recommending patience for the latter and humility for the former. On the same topic Ayala comments: "Also it is necessary that he who is to govern first know well how to govern himself; he who doesn't do this, should never take the position of correcting others or even admonishing them" (326). Much of the doctrinal themes is found in those verses that treat of advice and maxims, including such topics as inner peace and deception by worldly things and delights.[9] Ayala says that one's inner peace is lost in proportion to one's lack of charity toward others. He proceeds to list biblical examples of persons who committed some wrong because they did not have peace in their hearts—Cain, Absalom, and Judas. Referring to Judas Ayala says "If there had been peace in that traitor Judas, he would never have thought of selling the Lord; the devil can never be an inhabitant in a house where there is peace, harmony and Christian love" (541). The poet comments that it does not matter how much one fasts, prays, listens to masses and sermons, and gives alms to the poor; if you do not have peace in your heart, you are in danger and serious trouble.

The Great Schism

The first of three references to the schism in the *Rimado* deals with its origins in 1378. In both the *Rimado* and in the chronicles Ayala maintains a posture of neutrality. His criticism of the popes lies in the comparison of the first saintly popes, who felt unworthy to accept Saint

Peter's role and who ended up as martyrs, with those who "now have fist fights to see who will be pope" (197 d). He does not choose either of the popes, but he recognizes that the pope in Rome, Urban VI, was duly elected by all the cardinals. In the *Rimado*, Ayala makes only a brief reference to the public pressure and fear that the cardinals say they experienced: "Because in it there was force and public coercion" (200 c). The scene, as dramatized in year 1378, chapter 8, of the chronicle of Enrique II, is one of the most vivid in the chronicles (see the discussion in chapter 4). Ayala's suggestion that the division be settled by means of a council is not surprising in view of his strong advocacy of councilar government seen so clearly in the chronicles of Juan I and Enrique III.

The second reference to the schism (820–46) reveals a greater emotional involvement on the part of the poet. It is impressive to note that Ayala compares the pain and sadness that the ever-widening schism causes him, to the suffering he endured in prison. Twenty years have passed since the beginning of the schism. It is 1398 and the two contenders are Pedro de Luna (Benedict XIII) of Avignon and Boniface IX. King Enrique III held a meeting of Castilian churchmen in 1397 at which time it was decided to renounce obedience to Pedro de Luna and call for the election of only one pope. Ayala describes the state of the church at this time by means of the extended metaphor of the ship of Saint Peter (see the discussion below). The third reference (847–62) deals with events in 1403 when Enrique III, who has come of age, decides independently that Castile will once again give obedience to Pope Benedict XIII. The independent action by the young king permits Ayala to end this section on a somewhat more optimistic note by viewing the young king as the possible bearer of a solution to the division in the church.

Literary Aspects

Too often the true literary value or appreciation of a work is obscured because of comparisons with other works whose authors had different motives and purposes. Such has been the case of Ayala whose poem, *Rimado de Palacio,* is generally compared to the other great fourteenth-century poem in *cuaderna vía*, the *Libro de buen amor*. In addition to the predominant verse form, perhaps the most pertinent analogies between the two works are that both have a quasi-autobiographical character and both contain social criticism. Whereas the message of the *Libro de buen amor* and its author's intent have been debated for centuries, Ayala is an artist who always has a clear purpose for both the content and the form of his work. He does not write for amusement or diversion but rather to convey a serious message, principally concerning the state of the nation, the church, or his own soul. Ayala has chosen clarity of expression and didactic effectiveness rather than striving for more decorative and aesthetically pleasing verse. A somber and pessimistic tone pervades the *Rimado*. The didactic-moral nature of the work undoubtedly explains to some degree the prosaic style of portions of the poem. The choice of a formal, even rigid versification like *cuaderna vía* is appropriate to the author's purposes. As in the chronicles, Ayala's strength is in the effective use and arrangement of elements, in this case primarily nouns and verbs. His poetry gives an impression of sobriety and forcefulness instead of decorative beauty or virtuosity. His narrative poetry contains particularly effective use of satire and of dialogue, which enlivens and produces passages of impressive verisimilitude.

In assessing the *Rimado,* one must also consider the versification as well as other literary aspects. In the introduction to his critical edition of the work, Garcia presents an extensively detailed and convincing study of the versification of all parts of the poem. The conclusions drawn from his data give further evidence of a literary artist who is very aware of the subtleties of his craft. Ayala's versification not only proves to be very regular, but the change from seven to eight syllables in the hemistiches has a definite purpose and function. Although the *cuaderna vía* is suitable for Ayala's aims, it has the disadvantage of creating a sense of monotony by its very regularity and predictability. Therefore, it is the *cancionero* (732–919) that provides the most convincing and abundant evidence of the poet's domination of other forms. The arrangement of rhymes as well as the placement of the poems themselves is impressive evidence of poetic sensitivity. Garcia ends his remarks on versification by referring to Ayala's technical skill and then concludes: "The composition of the whole is exemplary."[10] Moreover, it is in the *cancionero* where some of the most effective examples of metaphorical language are found. This type of language comprises metaphors, allegories, similes, and epithets. In addition, the *Rimado* makes use of those poetic devices that are classified as "figures of construction," including cumulative effect, negatives, and repetition.

Cumulative Effect

In keeping with the didactic and moral intent of the poet, one sees
the need for rhetorical devices or techniques that will reinforce, underline,
stress, and repeat ideas. The greater part of the *Rimado* brings to mind
a sermon in which the preacher, because of the oral-aural nature of his
delivery, must try to fix certain ideas in the minds of his audience. In
order to do so the speaker will first make use of more external devices
such as alliteration, repetition, antithesis, order, parallelism, negatives,
and accumulation. Ayala, therefore, in much the same manner as a
preacher, avails himself of many of these devices, especially of those
that deal with word order. Irrespective of the poet's choice of vocabulary,
the effective ordering of words, whether plain or decorative, can not
only reinforce, but also enhance, the effect, particularly if the poem is
heard, rather than read silently. Frequently there appears in the *Rimado*
a cumulative effect by the actual piling up of terms, generally nouns
or adjectives, which may or may not be synonymous. For example, in
his discussion of the Ten Commandments, the poet explains how he
sinned to break a commandment. "Against this I sinned, Lord, every
day / believing in omens, erring in a serious way / in dreams and
sneezes and other astrology, / because all is vanity, madness and folly"
(22).[11] In addition to the emphasis on different superstitions, there is
also the accumulation of the three nouns that characterize somewhat
further the kind of sin committed. In the original Spanish, an added
feature to the cumulative effect is the mono-rhyme and the pause
between the hemistiches of each line:

> Contra esto pequé,   Señor, de cada día,
> creyendo en agüeros,   con grant malicia mía,
> en sueños e estornudos   e otra estrellería,
> ca todo es vanidat,   locura e follía.
>
> (22)

The alliterative effect of *sueños, estornudos* y *estrellería* also adds to the
overall impression.

A different context for the cumulative effect is the satire of the bad
wine which the landowners sell to the townsfolk: "the wine was sour,
cloudy, very bad, worthless, / whoever passes by and drinks it will
never go back there" (265 cd). It is significant that the adjectives are

grouped in two pairs, one relating to the objective and easily distin-
guishable physical characteristics. The two words in the other pair are
nearly synonymous and refer to the wine in more subjective, evaluative
terms. At any rate, Ayala's description leaves a lasting impression of
the taste and appearance that are usually associated with an inferior
wine. Another example of the cumulative effect is exemplified in Job's
lament to God that all of his friends have left him and passed over
him like a flood, concluding with this thought: "and very helpless /
I was left troubled, sad, poor, disconsolate" (974 cd). The image of
the flood comes from Job, but Ayala has added the series of five
adjectives that greatly intensifies the impression of his emotional state.
In the following stanza, the poet takes the word "wounds" from his
source and intensifies it by adding "tribulations." Job continues that
he is not asking his friends for their properties, and Ayala adds "nor
goods," another synonymous term. The overall effect is to emphasize
and bring more attention to Job's plight.

Negatives

Closely resembling the cumulative or piling up effect is the use of
several negatives usually within one stanza. Often the negatives appear
before single words, or before groups of words, thereby producing a
cumulative effect of negation. If read aloud, the repetitive negation
makes a strong impact upon the mind and memory of the listener.
The following description or definition of benign charity demonstrates
this effect: "not being covetous, / nor doing wrong to anyone, nor to
be at all proud / neither does it seek anything from others, nor is it
bad in itself / nor does it become enraged because of anger, except
for a just cause" (1755). The original Spanish version reveals more
sharply this negative effect: "La caridat veniña es non ser cobidciosa,
/ nin fazer mal *a ninguno,* nin *punto* orgullosa, / nin demanda lo
ajeno, nin en sí es maliciosa, / nin se ensaña *por ira,* salvo por justa
cosa." The Spanish version produces a stronger effect because it contains
more negative words and has a large number of reinforcing *n* and *m*
sounds. The italicized words are items which Ayala added to the biblical
original. They consist of three different types of intensifiers: *a ninguno*—
an additional negative; *punto*—a very minute amount; and *por ira*—a
synonymous expression.

In another example, Baldach informs his friend Job that his calamity
"was just and reasonable since [Job] did not have with him neither

patience nor serenity, neither comfort nor help" (1007 cd). Through use of the single nouns preceded by negatives, the resultant effect, especially if the passage is read aloud, is that of rapid repetition of the negative elements resembling a staccatolike rhythm. The Spanish *non* occurs only once in the passage but it is reinforced by the appearance three times of the word or syllable *con,* plus ending the first hemistich with *razón* which reinforces the sound. The negative *nin* is repeated three times also. Obviously such a device aids in fixing the main idea in the memories of the listeners or even readers. One of the most effective examples of this phenomenon is this passage inspired by an idea from the *Morals:* "Often man because of natural weakness / after he gains something good, doesn't value it as such / nor does one know who it is, nor what is good nor what is bad, / nor what will be better, nor what is a mortal thing" (1575). Again, just as in the previous example, here the enumeration, the shorter negative phrases, and the series of question words produce the attention-getting rapid rhythm along with the cumulative negative effect. Although Ayala's use of negatives is usually confined to individual stanzas, there are a few cases of negatives placed at the beginning of the first lines of several stanzas in a series. For example, in stanzas 605, 606, and 608, each first line respectively begins "Non deve el juez. . . . Non deve el juez. . . . Non deve ser cruel" (605 a, 606 a, 608 a). The English translation only partially conveys the overall sensation of the rhythmic negative effect: "The judge must not. . . . The judge must not. . . . He must not be cruel." In addition to the parallel negative effect of each first line, there is also the contrasting or opposite suggestion in each stanza that stresses affirmatively what each judge and public official should do.

Repetition

As discussed above, Ayala finds certain devices and techniques very compatible to his didactic-moralizing-sermonizing posture. Certainly the variety of examples that fall in the category of repetition is very extensive in the *Rimado de Palacio.* However, unlike, for example, the *Milagros* of Berceo, the *Rimado* has relatively few cases of simple or direct duplication or repetition of the same word in contiguous position. What one does find is the repetition of single words and phrases in different lines or hemistiches within an individual stanza. In a more limited distribution, there may be repetition involving two or more stanzas, as in the case of the last example of negation. Or there may be two or more types of repetition within an individual stanza. The following stanza depicting preparations for war demonstrates some of these characteristics: "They assemble galley slaves, they assemble crossbowmen / and oxen and carts, and other pikemen, / and to make stone projectiles, there come the stonecutters, / and they send to Burgos to call out the engineers" (517). Following the repetition of the verb "assemble," there are five examples of the conjunction "and," linking first nouns and then verb phrases. Although the use of many conjunctions within long sentences or phrases in prose was customary during this time, the effect in shorter phrases or lines of poetry is noteworthy. In addition to the usual objective of repetition as an attention and retention device, it is also ironic that the hemistiches along with the conjunctions serve to contrast somewhat the slaves, animals, and inanimate objects on the one hand against the skilled men on the other.

Another example of repetition, although much different in tone and theme, is a *copla* (verse or stanza) from the poem "Ave María" which forms part of Ayala's *Cancionero:* "Blessed are you the mother who conceived God, / blessed are you the woman who gave birth to such a son / blessed are you the maiden who was never corrupted, / blessed and praised are you who gave us such a son" (761). In spite of the obvious source for this *copla,* it is significant that the poet has constructed an architecturally balanced and effective unit through repetition and parallelism. The main adjective "blessed" is stressed at the beginning of each line and by the addition of "and praised" in the last line. Further parallels are the three titles bestowed upon Mary, the word "who" that begins the second hemistich of each line, and the repetition of "such a son" in identical position in the second and fourth lines. A structure similar to the above example, although much simpler in thought, is the following which treats of the Great Schism. The time alluded to in this passage is the year 1398 when it was decided that both popes, Boniface IX and Benedict XIII, should reign and allow a general council to elect one pope only: "Whether he be French, whether from Hungary, / whether from Spain, whether German, / whether he be English, or from Lombardy, / whether he be Scotch, whether Catalonian" (839 a–d). By repeating the word "whether" at the beginning of each half line or hemistich, the poet emphasizes the equality of each nation. At the same time he confirms their insignificance in global terms when he adds: "as long as he is Christian" (839 e). In spite of its prosaic quality, the stanza effectively conveys the poet's message.

Stanzas 528 and 1102 are significantly similar with respect to the type of repetition demonstrated as well as in content. In praise of peace Ayala writes: "This [peace] makes the poor man reach a great height; / Peace makes it so the rich man can enjoy his riches; / this punishes the evildoer without any delay; / This makes the good man's fortitude last" (528). And in the following example Job discusses the omnipotence of God: "This one brings the powerful down to the ground, / This one makes the peace and prevents war, / This one makes the plains, the woodlands and the mountains, / This one is he who pardons the sinner if he errs" (1102). In the first example the repeated word "This" referring to peace produces the concept of a person or a dynamic entity who has the capability of accomplishing so many things as also indicated by the repeated verb "makes." The second example has a stronger crescendo effect as the wonderful powers of "This one" increase in each consecutive line, finally reaching a series of three in the third line. The fourth line is the highest point of the crescendo because it is so personal and because it contrasts with the panoramic sweep of the previous concepts. Another type of repetition, the polyptoton, a traditional device used in the *Libro de buen amor* and in the works of Berceo, appears very rarely in the *Rimado*.[12] Generally the examples of polyptotons in the *Rimado* are found within individual lines of a stanza and usually reflect different tenses of a verb: "Thus it happens, cursed sin!, and it happened and it will happen" (336 c); "I mourn mourning, because I ought to mourn" (846 a); and in reference to the Virgin Mary: "because this one protects, protected and would protect me" (865 c). The repetition and alliteration that characterize the polyptoton as revealed in these examples achieve different effects, such as a sense of completeness, finality, authority, or assertiveness.

Figurative Language

Many of the metaphors in the *Rimado* are relatively short, frequently comprising a few lines or at most a stanza. A graphic description of the king who is faced with the problem of paying his soldiers who threaten to burn and loot the towns is presented in this manner: "The king goes around in silence / It seems that he is a bull who is being goaded" (491 ab). By comparing the king to a goaded bull, one senses the feeling of helplessness and silent fury of the king who is the object of complaints or barbs from all sides about the soldiers' behavior. The image of the bull is particularly effective as the previous stanza deals with a complaint by the farmers. In another passage, a king is pleased with himself and is especially grateful to the Jewish tax collectors who have imposed higher taxes on the people that year. The poet continues: "the sufferer does not notice / that all of this blood is coming out of his side" (253 cd). One interpretation is the comparison of blood, an essential life-giving and sustaining substance, to money. Because Ayala has been referring to the Jewish tax collectors, and also because of the site of the wound, the allusion to the crucifixion is apparent. It is highly possible that Ayala had the King Pedro I in mind when he writes about the active participation of the Jews during that reign. A possible allusion to Pedro I is also made in this stanza: "Because the king kills men they don't call him just, / for it would be a false name but a more appropriate one is butcher. / For the very noble justice has its true name / The noonday sun and the morning star" (348). By using the term butcher, the poet further condemns the actions of a king who seemingly kills men indiscriminately and by a crude and heartless manner. The idea of justice being noble also suggests a just king whose admirable character is metaphorically described by the traditional symbols of sun and star which equate such attributes as truth, purity, goodness, and honor.

The metaphor of man as a leaf is presented in two different passages, stanzas 1111 and 1834–35. In the first example, man's weakness and vulnerability to death are represented by a leaf that is tossed about by a mere light wind and eventually the leaf dies. Job makes this analogy to prove to God that he should not consider him an enemy because after all he is merely a mortal. However, in the second example the metaphor is extended and explained more fully. Now Job explains that man, the leaf, has fallen because of his sin from the tree of paradise. In addition to the general idea of falling from grace, Job describes the wind as being first a robber wind and second a wind of temptation. Both examples underline the helpless and fickle nature of man, although the second example further explains the temptations and motivations as "weak and base desires" (1835 d). Again, with respect to the first example, the analogy of man and a leaf is a clear example of the normal life span of an individual and suggests by extension the seasons, a traditional means of representing the stages of man. Ayala faithfully reflects his source in stanzas 1834–35. His poetic contribution is primarily in putting the ideas into verse form. In stanza 1111, on the other hand, Ayala's poetic rendering is different from the lines in Job in tone and emphasis. Job's challenging, complaining tone is gone, and his question: "Why do you hide your face from me and consider me an enemy?" becomes an humble supplication. Ayala pleads: "Oh Lord, your face, do not hide it from me / nor as an enemy judge me against thee" (1111 ab). The first line begins with "Oh Señor" and ends with the word "mí," and the second line ends with "Ti." The position of the words gives them prime importance, and the rhyme in stressed "í" is particularly appropriate to convey his personal suffering. The negatives that begin the second and third hemistiches are reinforced by two more negative words in the first half of the third line. This is effective in stressing the poet's feeling of unworthiness as he seeks reconciliation with his Lord.

One of Ayala's favorite themes is the temporary and transient nature of worldly goods and pleasures often presented by metaphorical language. On the subject of wealth, Ayala gives the following comparisons: "All of the riches are mist and dew, / the honors and pride and that wild enthusiasm; / man goes to bed healthy and at dawn he is cold, / because our life runs, like the water of the river" (271). The transitory character of wealth and glory is likened to the short-lived mist, which soon lifts and disappears in the morning, and the dew, which again appears early at dawn and then dries as the sun warms the earth. Also, the diaphanous nature of mist suggests a transparency, a lack of substance, or a shallowness of worldly things. Another aspect of the dew is its sparkling clear beauty which first appears rather early and then vanishes, a reference again to the transient nature of such earthly values as beauty. The adjectives "healthy" and "cold" obviously represent, respectively, life and death.

Among Ayala's longer and more developed metaphors, which in this case can be called an allegory, is the famous "Ship of Saint Peter," representing the Catholic church and in this context, the time of the Great Schism:[13]

> The ship of Saint Peter is going through a great storm,
> no one thinks about going to help her.
> From thirteen hundred and seventy eight
> until now I have seen her suffering greatly,
> and he who can help her doesn't want to help,
> And so she is about to be sunk
> if God doesn't help this time,
> according to his custom, without our deserving it.
>   (830)

I see great swells and a frightful wave,
the vast high sea, the split mast.
She doesn't find a safe port where she can moor,
her rudder is weakened.
Now that she has been forgotten by the sailors,
the sturdy anchors are of no use to her,
in fact her boards broken by force, and
all help from the ropes seems lost.

(831)

. . . .

When Apostle Peter feared he would perish
being in the sea in the little boat,
because of the great wind which he saw was getting stronger,
he called out to God in a very loud voice:
"Lord, we are perishing, please don't forsake
these poor servants of yours" and his plea
was soon heard because of his devotion
and thus the storm was ended.

(834)

I understand the waves to be pride and covetousness
which cause that ship to sink,
and the syllogisms and argumentation
are also waves for arguing stubbornly.

(835 a–d)

In the first stanza the poet refers to the schism as the great storm
through which the ship of Saint Peter is passing. The last two lines of
stanza 830 reflect the medieval Christian attitude of humility and
submission to the divine will. In the next stanza, 831, Ayala sets up
a balanced equation of groups of noun and adjective in each hemistich
of the first two lines. These lines refer back to the "storm" at the end
of the first line of stanza 1, and then continue with the metaphor.
Ayala reflects his own experience and emphasizes his interest and concern
over the schism by establishing his role of observer within the poem.
It also gives a sense of immediacy and urgency to an event that had
dragged on for decades. In keeping with the medieval tradition, the
extended metaphor of the first two stanzas is explained and deciphered
systematically in the next two. In the description of the ship, the poet
mentions those parts that are basic and vital for its safety and maneu-

verability—mast, rudder, anchors, boards, cables. Each of these parts contribute to the extended metaphor or allegory of the sinking ship of St. Peter. Also, Ayala associates each ship feature with a segment of the organization of the church, assessing the importance of each in direct proportion to the value of the ship feature. Therefore, it is logical that the rudder should represent the pope and the mast should represent the College of Cardinals. The choice of the anchors to represent the Christian kings, the princes of the church, is indeed effective inasmuch as the anchors suggest the potential and ability of the princes to help solve the problem and at least stabilize the ship, but unfortunately, they have withdrawn their support.

After identifying the metaphors with the church hierarchy, there follows a commentary on the long period of chaos and suffering with a dual reference in stanza 833 to the sea of life and the stormy sea, the plight of the church. Instead of pausing to make a direct plea to God for help, the poet makes an indirect invocation in the fifth stanza by recalling the exemplum of the Apostle Peter faced with the threat of perishing on the sea in his small boat. Peter's devotion, which caused his voice to be heard by the Lord, contrasts with the sins expressed in the next stanza. The allegory is remarkably complete even to the point of characterizing the waves as symbolic of pride and avarice or representing the forms of debate or dialectics that have impeded any resolution to the problem of the schism. Perhaps just as noteworthy as the effective imagery and well-conceived metaphors is the unity of the entire allegory as demonstrated in the linking and development of associated ideas or symbols. To further emphasize its importance, Ayala chose the twelve syllable *arte mayor* as the meter and placed the poem in the center of his *cancionero*.

In order to describe how sins may snare unsuspecting souls, Ayala uses the sport of fishing to represent the above action metaphorically. One possible source for this theme is the *Libro de buen amor* in which Juan Ruiz describes how Trotaconventos, the go-between, or men, in a metaphorical sense, bait their hooks to catch the innocent and unsuspecting young women.[14] Ayala develops the fishing metaphor in the following manner: "Everywhere sins have the hooks, / with which the souls fish for their tears and sorrows: / wherever we pass the ground is full / of the parents and grandparents sown by the enemy" (174). Several ideas or elements comprise the extended metaphor of fishing. For example, the reference to hooks envisions luring the unsuspecting or gullible souls. Then, too, perhaps the idea of the souls

fishing for their own perdition indicates lack of prudence or willpower
on the part of these souls to either heed warnings or resist temptation.
The third line refers to the ground being covered with fish that have
been caught. The reference in line 4 to sowing and to ancestors adds
another dimension to the concept of line 3, now referring to those who
are dead and buried—victims of the devil. Moreover, the reference to
sowing suggests the replenishing of the supply of future victims.

Another extended metaphor or allegory Ayala develops well is that
of the ladder demonstrating the caution and prudence that a king's
confidential advisor must have in order to survive in the court.[15] The
exemplum is about a prince who plans to besiege a city and has placed
a ladder next to the wall so that the armed men could climb up and
get into the city. One man examines carefully the ladder to determine
whether it is sturdy and whether it would pose any problem or danger.
Having determined that the ladder was quite strong and safe, the man
next wondered if the ladder just reached the top of the wall or if it
were taller than he had estimated. Also, the man wanted to be certain
that responsible and trustworthy persons would accompany him on the
ladder. Ayala presents the metaphor in stanzas 658–62. The explanation
of the images is more than four times as long, lasting over twenty
stanzas. The ascent of the ladder is likened to what Ayala considers
the dangerous entry into the circle of royal court advisors. The author's
concern about whether the king was too young, inexperienced, or
unpredictable relates most closely to the minority of Enrique III. In
addition, Ayala was aware of the problems during the minority of
Alfonso XI and the early years of Pedro I, who ascended the throne
at sixteen. The ladder itself represents the king, whereas the length of
it corresponds to the advisor's ambition and abilities.

In one of the poems entitled "Tristura e grant cuidado" (Sadness
and great worry) which is found in the *Cancionero,* the poet develops
the theme of four emotions that are presented allegorically—sadness,
worry, pleasure, and joy.

> Sadness and great Worry
> are ever at my side,
> Since Pleasure and Joy
> have abandoned me like this.
> (783—refrain)
>
> They have abandoned me
> without my deserving such treatment from them,

because I always loved Pleasure,
and I was satisfied with Joy,
and now, because of my sin,
they turned their wrath against me,
in this strange land
they left me forgotten.
                    (784)

They left me forgotten
in a dark prison,
where Worry and Sadness
found me very grief-stricken;
since they saw me isolated,
They never leave my side:
since that time up to now
I am accompanied by them.
                    (786)

I am accompanied by them
and my sad heart
always and at every moment
they have guarded well;
and I see that if I permit them
they will never leave my side
and they will dwell with me,
as long as I live, troubled!
                    (788)

The refrain or *estribillo* (in alternate stanzas, that is, in 783, 785, 787, etc.) states the poet's present emotional state with the allegorical pair of Sadness and Worry who have taken the places of the past emotions of Pleasure and Joy. The poem is unified both structurally and thematically. The beginning refrain is repeated after every stanza. Moreover, the last line of the refrain is duplicated as the first line of stanza 1. The last line of each stanza is repeated as the first line of the following stanza. The rhyme of the refrain is *abba* and in the other stanzas *acca adda*. The repetition of the rhyme also adds to the sense of unity. The four emotions are introduced in the refrain. The accompaniment by the first two contrasts with the abandonment of the second pair. The first *copla* is devoted to Pleasure and Joy; in the second, they exchange places with Sadness and Worry, which then dominate the final *copla*. There is sufficient evidence to believe that many of the references in this poem are autobiographical and thereby lend a sincere tone to the poet's picture of grief and sadness. For example, "this strange land," although somewhat exaggerated, may refer to Portugal where Ayala was imprisoned. Also, the allusion to a "dark prison" again may refer to the poet's imprisonment in the castle of Obidos.

Similes

In comparison to the metaphors and allegories, most of the similes in the *Rimado* are short, hardly ever comprising more than two lines of verse. Much of the biblical material in the *Rimado* based on the *Morals* and the Book of Job is expressed in figurative language with a large percentage containing similes. Ayala's satire of society and government is also enhanced by the effective use of this technique. For example, Ayala criticizes the prelates, who, motivated by worldly gain, frequent the court instead of supervising their churches, and "they help to stir up the kingdom as much as possible, / just as thrushes stir up the miserable pigeon house" (246 cd). With the exception of some technical theological terms, Ayala's lexicon, even for his imagery, contains many expressions that are peculiar to a rural or agricultural society. This is another reflection of his attachment to his home area of Alava.

Further commentary on the corruption and the wretched condition of the masses describes those conditions, which "for the wretched people were black like coal" (252 b). The exodus of many people from the areas of high taxation is described in this manner: "Where a thousand men used to dwell, no longer dwell there three hundred; / more taxes than hailstones fall down upon them; / the small ones and the large ones flee because of such penalties, / for now they are burned alive without fire and without vine shoots" (261). Ayala creates a provocative plastic picture with the imagery of hailstones falling from above and the metaphorical allusion of the fire and vine shoots, and the "burning" to represent the plight of the taxpayers. In addition to the simile of the hailstones, there is also the contrasting juxtaposition of fire and hailstones which are a form of water. By extension, these elements suggest punishment from above and below, or perhaps the idea of hell on earth. It is interesting that the poet who comes from the region of La Rioja, refers to the vine shoots which are not only used for kindling, but also give a delicious flavor to the outdoor roastings. The reference to the "small ones" and the "large ones" is an indirect manner of identifying the poor and the rich. Many virtues are developed in the

Rimado by the use of figurative language usually in the form of metaphors or similes. For example, justice is one of the virtues that is highly esteemed by the poet, who likens it to a star that shines so brightly (345 b) or, as Ayala affirms passionately, "I love justice as though I were burning with fire" (363 d). Other examples of similes are found in the epithets to the Virgin and the treatment of such topics as life and death.

Names or Epithets Assigned to the Virgin

Many examples of names or epithets assigned to the Virgin are found in the *Rimado*. The *Cancionero* contains several Marian poems as well as poems dedicated to God. Some of the names assigned to the Virgin suggest metaphorically the different roles and attributes that attest to her greatness and popularity. Because of the portrayal of the Virgin as a mediator and savior, many of the epithets suggest her role as being that of an epic heroine. The title of Virgin Mary, the most frequent and perhaps the most well recognized name for her, is expressive of the immaculate conception. Some variations or modifications of Virgin Mary are the "Holy Virgin Mary" (752 a), "Forever Virgin and Maiden" (758 c), "Very Holy Virgin" (779 b), "Holy Virgin" (874 b), and "Virgin Worthy of Honor" (910 c). Often the Virgin is simply called "Lady" or "My Lady" (735 b) along with more qualified designations such as "Merciful Lady" (767 c), "My Very Kind Lady" (774 a), "Perfect Lady" (908 b), "My Sweet Lady" (806 b), or "Very Glorious Lady" (767 a). References to Mary as the "Mother of God" also abound in such variations as "Very Noble Mother" (753 b) and "Glorious Mother" (806 a). The adjective "glorious" may be coupled with many nouns, as for example, Lady, Virgin, Mary, and Queen. Variants for the latter designation include "Precious Queen of Great Worth" (755 a) and "Noble Queen of Valor" (910 b).

Frequently metaphorical expressions will make the implied comparison to the Virgin as "courage and comfort" (755 b), "very sweet medicine" (814 a), "comfort of the troubled" (889 a), and "blanket and shawl of sinners" (874 f). The above expressions seem to identify more closely the virtues and capabilities of the Virgin especially with respect to her different roles. One important role of the Virgin is that of mediator or in a broad sense helper. Usually the Virgin is invoked in prayer as in the following lyrical stanza: "Lady, may you help me, Holy Virgin Mary / to whom I always commend myself night and day, / and be my helper and my mediator *(abogada)*, / and to your blessed son, / plead for me and say: / Give me that servant who calls me every day, / because I heard his tearful prayers" (752). In another stanza she is called "key to paradise" (863 e).

Sometimes the troubled sinners pray to the Virgin seeking her guidance and help by comparing her to a star: "You who are the star" (818 a), "Lady, shining star" (867 a), "Star of the sea" (872 a), and "star of the lost ones" (889 c). The comparison of the Virgin to a star clearly implies the role of guide, one whose light shows the way to the lost or instructs or shows the strayed or the ignorant. With the last concept, the star emitting its brilliant light suggests understanding, revelation, and truth. An instance of the Virgin as guide is shown in the following refrain: "Lady, shining star / who guides everybody, / guide this one your servant, / who entrusts his soul to you" (867). A different emphasis on the personal attributes of the Virgin includes two metaphors that allude to the virginity of Mary "the closed door" (876 a) and the "closed garden" (878 a). According to the prophecy of Ezequiel, the door, which represents Mary's virginity, may only be opened to receive God and give birth to his son.[16] In addition to the comparisons of the Virgin's beauty to trees, beautiful flowers, and sweet-smelling plants are also likened to her as for example, the rose: "You are the flower of flowers, you, the rose of the roses" (767 b).[17] In the above comparisons the Virgin Mary represents the paragon of all flowers including the beautiful rose.

On Life, Death, and Similar Topics

Topics or themes in the *Rimado* pertaining to life, death, and the passage of time, in spite of presenting traditional medieval ideas, are frequently expressed with effective imagery or metaphorical language. Throughout the *Rimado* the poet often combines the topics of life and death, as reflected in the idea of life being a journey toward death or the idea of our lives being like small rivers that end up in the sea of death. Life on earth is viewed as brief and transient, and generally characterized by suffering and sin. Each day is considered a day's march toward death, which is destined and therefore inescapable. Although it may seem as though our life is being extended, one should merely think of that time in negative terms, as being subtracted from our total life span. The concept of the inequality of life in contrast to the equality of death is presented in one stanza as follows: "To the good and the bad, life is unequal: / one prospers, it's very bad for another; /

afterwards death comes which is equal for all, / and worms cover them and nothing can help them" (1187). Several passages similar to the above describe the grim aspects of physical death, characterized by the stench coming from the graves or referring to the effects of rigor mortis: "you will see the dead statue, cold, and without color" (1821 cd). In this stanza and the following one, the familiar form of address used by the speaker is very effective as he refers to the person who used to go around puffed up with pride, but now "you'll see him where he lies decayed and buried, / for there is no difference between the poor and the rich, / except that the sepulcher will look better" (1822 cd). The poet was inspired by the concepts in the *Morals* and in Job, but the more graphic or colorful details and the tone of the passages were added by Ayala himself. Some of the metaphorical expressions used to represent life include shadows that may disappear without leaving any trace just as some lives that have been unimportant and have had little effect on others.

Reference to hell and the devil are usually traditional and reminiscent of the euphemisms found in other contemporary works. Hell is generally represented by fire such as "in the lasting fire which is always burning" (58 a), "the lit fire" (392 d), or "that bad fire" (564 d). The devil is described as the chief or leader *(caudillo)* of the darkness. From the belief that one who does bad things abhors light and loves darkness, it follows and is fitting that "he deserves to see darkness always, / and with the chief of darkness such a sinner should perish" (312). One of the more graphic accounts of hell and especially the devil describes the torments and tortures that the condemned must suffer in hell. There are horrible beasts and frightening serpents with their mouths twisted into ferocious leers and gnashing their teeth to remind the condemned of their evil deeds on earth. Also, the poor souls are continually tormented by a large host of devils numbering in the thousands (571–73).

A representative combination of Ayala's thoughts on life and death is found in *coplas* 565–68. The predominant note in these lines is the *ubi sunt* theme with lesser emphasis on the other traditional views of life and death. It is significant that Ayala's *coplas* precede the famous elegy by Jorge Manrique, *Coplas a la muerte de su padre,* by almost a century:

> What happened then to the rich man and to his power
> to his vainglory, and to his proud spirit?

All is now passed and ran like the river,
and of all his planning only the great cold was left.

Where are the many years that we have endured
in this bad world wretched and unhappy?
Where are the elegant dresses of finely decorated cloth?
Where are the goblets and glasses of very priceless metal?

Where are the large country estates and houses?
the villas and castles, the crenellated towers,
the flocks of sheep, the numerous cows,
the spirited horses of the golden saddles,

the pleasant sons and his numerous flocks,
the woman greatly loved, the treasure collected,
the relatives and brothers who had accompanied him?
In a very bad cave. All have left him.
(565–68)

The first stanza begins with a question about a person who represents the most privileged and most secure group—the rich. He is characterized by power, vainglory, and pride. The last two lines of the stanza answer the question: everything ends with the inevitable coming of "the great cold," that is, death. The second stanza begins with the first of a series of "Where are" questions. It is somewhat unusual in the implication that the suffering of this world also passes and is, in the end, of little importance. The series of questions regarding the rich man's possessions and family that follows is effectively presented, with much variation in use of repetition and parallelism. The questions are again answered in the last line with another image of death. The last phrase of the stanza, "all have left him," because of its position intensifies the sense of absolute isolation and abandonment.

Influence of the *Rimado* on Later Poetry and Poets

One of the highlights of the *Rimado de Palacio* is the portrayal of the society and customs of the fourteenth century. The scenes of court life, having their basis in personal experience and observation, have quite rightly been accorded much notice and high praise for their vigor and accuracy.[18]

Ayala's description of personages in the royal courts, the almost caricaturelike presentation of merchants and lawyers, prefigure later satirical works that culminate in the mordant sarcasm and ridicule of Quevedo, as well as in subsequent *cuadros de costumbres* (vignettes of manners and customs). Ayala demonstrates originality in his combining confessional and doctrinal themes and materials based on the Bible and the *Morals* of Saint Gregory in order to produce a didactic exposition in verse. E. B. Strong, commenting on Ayala's contribution observes: "Ayala's confession seems to have been the first of its kind in Castilian verse and may have served as a model for the rimed confessions of Fernán Pérez de Guzmán and Ruy Páez de Ribera."[19] Many of the themes, which reflect the stoicism of the fifteenth century, undoubtedly received some impetus from the meditations on life, death, original sin, and the brief duration of worldly gains as portrayed in the *Rimado*. In several respects, Ayala has proved to be an innovator, in spite of the fact that he was the last of the *cuaderna vía* poets. These innovations include the increased use of the eight-syllable line and the introduction of *arte mayor,* both of which are most apparent in the *Cancionero* portion of the *Rimado*. In addition to verse forms, he influenced the topics and themes of later poets. His devout and deeply moving poems dedicated to the Virgin also made an impressive impact on religious lyrical poetry of the fifteenth century.

Notes and References

Chapter One

1. See the following works for information on the history of fourteenth-century Spain: Claudio Sánchez Albornoz, *España un enigma histórico* (Buenos Aires, 1956); Rafael de Altamira, *A History of Spain* (New York, 1949); J. N. Hillgarth, *The Spanish Kingdoms, 1250–1516*, vol. 1 (Oxford, 1976); Angus MacKay, *Spain in the Middle Ages: From Frontier to Empire 1000–1500* (London, 1977); Joseph F. O'Callaghan, *A History of Medieval Spain* (Ithaca, 1975); P. E. Russell, *The English Intervention in Spain and Portugal in the Time of Edward III and Richard II* (Oxford, 1955); Luis Suárez Fernández, *El Canciller Pedro López de Ayala y su tiempo (1332–1407)* (Vitoria, 1962), *Castilla, el cisma y la crisis conciliar* (Madrid, 1960), and *Historia de España antigua y media*, 2 vols. (Madrid, 1976).

2. Kenneth Adams in the introduction to his edition of the *Rimado del Palacio* (Madrid, 1971), 8, notes that it is impossible to read Ayala's chronicles or poetry without relating them to the abundant available data pertinent to the chronicler's life.

See the following works for additional biographical data: Rafael Floranes, *Vida literaria del Canciller Mayor de Castilla don Pedro López de Ayala, restaurador de las letras en Castilla*, Documentos inéditos para la historia de España, vols. 19–20 (Madrid, 1851–52); Michel Garcia, *Obra y personalidad del Canciller Ayala* (Madrid, 1983); Marqués de Lozoya, *Biografía del Canciller don Pedro López de Ayala* (Vitoria, 1932); Franco Meregalli, *La vida política del Canciller Ayala* (Milan, 1955).

3. Adams, commenting on the complex labyrinth of documents that were studied to determine Ayala's nobility, concludes: "Ferdinand the Catholic would be the fifth generation grandson of Ayala's father" (*Rimado*, 9).

4. Floranes (*Vida*, 39–43) maintains that Ayala was brought up at home and that his uncle interested him in the life at court; see also Meregalli, *Vida*, 20.

5. *Generaciones y semblanzas*, ed. R. B. Tate (London, 1965), 15.

Chapter Two

1. The number of folios is based on British Library MS Add. 17906 because it contains all four chronicles in fairly complete form.

2. Garcia, *Obra*, 154, 171. Extensive investigation of the codices, including source studies, have been carried out for a number of years by Germán Orduna and his investigative team in Buenos Aires. Their research

promises to shed more light on many aspects of this complex manuscript tradition.

3. Pero López de Ayala, *Coronica del rey don Pedro,* ed. C. L. Wilkins and H. M. Wilkins (Madison, 1985), 20; hereafter cited in the text.

In this study all translations of quotations are my own. In translating Ayala's works, I have attempted to follow as closely as possible the vocabulary and style of old Spanish. Quotations of material from the other three chronicles come from BAE, vol. 68, and have been checked for accuracy against British Library MS add. 17906 and Academia de la Historia (Madrid) MS 9–4765. References in the text cite the abbreviation *BAE* and a page number.

4. The final chapters of the chronicle in some manuscripts deal exclusively with events in Avignon, beginning with the death of Pope Clement VII and the election to the papacy of Cardinal Pedro de Luna of Aragon, who took the name Benedict XIII.

Chapter Three

1. Rafael Lapesa, "El Canciller de Ayala y otros poetas del mester de clerecía," in *Historia general de las literaturas hispánicas,* ed. G. Díaz Plaja, vol. 1 (Barcelona, 1949), 497.

2. Robert B. Tate, *Ensayos sobre la historiografía peninsular del siglo XV* (Madrid, 1970), 37.

3. See Luis Suárez Fernández, *Juan I, Rey de Castilla (1379–1390)* (Madrid, 1955), 25.

4. For examples of Pedro's concern for chivalric conduct, see *Coronica,* ed. Wilkins, 431, 554.

5. See Suárez Fernández, *Juan I,* 8–9, and *Nobleza y monarquía* (Valladolid, 1959), 27.

6. The sultan refers to himself in equally glowing terms, such as "noble lord, just one, tender of the offended, insurer of pilgrim roads" (BAE, 81–82).

7. Ayala includes a variety of details that reveal the chronicler's interest in linguistic data, that is, the significance and derivation of words. See, for example, *Coronica,* ed. Wilkins, 21.

8. See Luis Vincente Díaz Martín, *Itinerario de Pedro I de Castilla* (Valladolid, 1975), 9–13.

9. See Russell, *English Intervention,* 229–35.

Chapter Four

1. See Alan Deyermond, *Historia de la literatura española: La Edad Media,* 4th ed. (Barcelona, 1978), 238–40.

2. See Richard P. Kinkade, "Pero López de Ayala and the Order of St. Jerome," *Symposium* 26, no. 2 (1972):169–70.

3. Latin rhetorical terms for these devices include *amplificatio, interpretatio, expolitio, aferre contrarium,* and *oppositio.*

4. Alberto Vàrvaro, "Pero López de Ayala: le Crónicas," in *Manuale di filologia spagnola medievale,* vol. 2, *Letteratura* (Naples, 1969), 184.

5. For additional dramatic episodes in the chronicle of Juan I see BAE, 66, 81, 86. In the chronicle of Enrique III see ibid., 184–85, 222–23, 229–30.

Chapter Five

1. Peter Russell, *English Intervention,* 21–22, observed that Queen Isabel disapproved of calling Pedro "Cruel." Also, Philip II ordered the changing of the title of Pedro's bust from "El Cruel" to "El Justiciero."

2. See Marcelino Menéndez y Pelayo, *Historia de la poesía castellana en la Edad Media,* vol. 1 (Madrid, 1911), 358, and Fueter, *Geschichte der neuren Historiographie* (Munich, 1911), 227.

3. See for example Deyermond, *Historia,* 266 and Hillgarth, *Spanish Kingdoms,* 373.

4. P. E. Russell, "The *Memorias* of Fernán Alvarez de Albornoz, Archbishop of Seville, 1371–80," in *Hispanic Studies in Honour of I. González Llubera,* ed. F. Pierce (Oxford, 1959), 319–330, comments on the enthusiasm and support of Fernán Alvarez for Enrique de Trastámara and the hostility of the church toward Pedro I. In spite of offering several new dates and correcting the date of Pedro's death, *Memorias* corroborates several events in the Ayala chronicle. Adams maintains that there is not sufficient documentation with which to accuse Ayala of having misrepresented the facts. Nor does he believe that propaganda is rampant in the chronicle with this supporting opinion: "it would have been quite easy for his contemporaries to recognize such distortions" (ibid., 13).

5. Angel Valbuena Prat, *Historia de la literatura española,* 7th ed. (Barcelona, 1963), 1:189.

6. Rafael Lapesa, "El Canciller de Ayala y otros poetas del mester de clerecía," in *Historia general de las literaturas hispánicas,* ed. G. Díaz Plaja, vol. 1 (Barcelona, 1949), 512.

7. See Angel del Río, *Historia de la literatura española,* rev. ed. (New York, 1963), 1:115.

8. See Tate, *Ensayos,* 48–52; see also the commentary of Cherrie Soper in the introduction to her anthology of Ayala chronicles, *Las crónicas* (Zaragoza, 1975), 17.

9. See for example Várvaro, "Pero López de Ayala," 184.

10. Tate, *Generaciones,* 15.

11. Livy's work originally comprised 142 books. Menéndez y Pelayo states that Ayala translated the *Decades,* books 1–2 and 4, during the last eight years of his life.

12. Marcelino Menéndez y Pelayo, ed., *Antología de poetas líricos castellanos* (Santander, 1944), 1:351.

13. Curt J. Wittlin, "Hacia una edición crítica de la traducción de las *Décadas* de Tito Livio hecha por Pero López de Ayala," *Revista Canadiense de Estudios Hispánicos* 1, no. 3 (1977):299.

14. Eric W. Naylor, "Pero López de Ayala's Translation of Boccaccio's *De Casibus*" in *Hispanic Studies in Honor of Alan D. Deyermond*, ed. John S. Miletich (Madison, 1986), 205–16. See also Lapesa, "El Canciller de Ayala," 496.

15. Kinkade, "Ayala and St. Jerome," 167.

16. *Libro de la caza de las aves*, José Fradejas Lebrero (Valencia, 1969), 52; hereafter cited in the text.

17. In Lebrero's edition (ibid.) the borrowed materials are printed in italics and Ayala's original writing appears in regular type. On the basis of page count, more than three fifths of the work was composed originally by Ayala.

18. Lapesa, "El Canciller," 512.

Chapter Six

1. See *Libro Rimado del Palacio*, ed. Jacques Joset (Madrid, 1978), 23, and Lapesa, *Libro*, 495–96.

2. I have used *"Libro de Poemas"* o *"Rimado de Palacio,"* ed. Michel Garcia, 2 vols. (Madrid, 1978), a well-prepared, scholarly critical edition with a textual apparatus that includes helpful explanatory notes. An index of words and phrases indicates the stanza in whose notes the words are explained. Volume 2 contains the text of the Book of Job and the *Morals* of St. Gregory, which served as models for stanzas 920–2168. Their inclusion in the text facilitates comparison of Ayala's adaptation and the source materials.

3. Helen L. Sears, "The Rimado de Palacio and the *De Regimine* Tradition of the Middle Ages," *Hispanic Review* 20 (1952):26. In addition to the works discussed by Sears, such sources as the *Historia Troyana* by Guido de Columna and the *Caída de Príncipes* by Boccaccio may have had some influence on Ayala's work.

4. Adams, ed., *Rimado*, observes that Ayala was evidently familiar with contemporary poetry and that he must have known works of *cuaderna vía*. Adams supports his belief that Ayala knew some of the current lyrical works by noting the poet's use of a variety of metrical forms and also a technical vocabulary including such terms as *canción, deitado,* and *versete.*

5. Garcia, in *Libro de Poemas*, makes the following observation: "This brief mention of the Amadís is the second that is known in Castilian literature, the first being that which Juan de Castrogeriz made in a gloss of the *De regimine principum*, published between 1345 and 1350" (127).

6. See ibid., 148, n. 234. Stanza 236 d, which alludes to throwing out an unjust king as well as references to Jewish court officials, are among the lines that support this suggestion.

7. See also the chronicle of Juan I (BAE, 139), where Ayala criticizes the manner of giving communion but in a less personal fashion.

8. Lapesa, "El Canciller," 505.

9. Lapesa (ibid., 507), referring to the last part of the *Rimado*, writes: "It is of interest, nevertheless, because of the criteria adopted on selecting it; that which has been selected pertains almost always to the historical exposition and its commentary; at times passages of moral interpretation are taken, but the allegorical part is cast aside."

10. Garcia, *Libro de Poemas*, 58.

11. Sneezes were considered good if one sneezed in the evening, bad when they occurred during the morning, and harmful on getting out of bed, or getting up from the table. See *El porqué de los dichos*, ed. José María Iribarren, 3d ed. (Madrid, 1962), 633.

12. Polyptoton is a rhetorical device in which a word is repeated in different cases, numbers, genders, and the like.

13. See Garcia, *Libro de Poemas*, 142, n. 212a. See also E. B. Strong, "Pero López de Ayala's Proposals for Ending the Great Schism," *Bulletin of Hispanic Studies* 38 (1961):64–77.

14. See stanzas 884 and 1537 in *Libro de buen amor*, ed. Joan Corominas (Madrid, 1967), 343, 583–85.

15. See stanzas 658–62. See also Richard P. Kinkade, "On Dating the *Rimado de Palacio*," *Kentucky Romance Quarterly* 18, no. 1 (1971):27.

16. See Song of Songs 4:12.

17. See Ecclesiastes 24:17–19.

18. See for example, Kinkade, "On Dating," 18, and del Río, *Historia*, 116.

19. E. B. Strong, "The *Rimado de Palacio*: López de Ayala's Rimed Confession," *Hispanic Review* 37 (1969):439. Rafael Lapesa refers to the new spirit in Ayala's verses of *cuaderna via* and the *zejel*, adding, "his versions and extracts of the *Morals* of Saint Gregory influenced notably the emphasis on religious topics of the immediate generation" (*La obra literaria del Marqués de Santillana* [Madrid, 1957], 16).

Selected Bibliography

PRIMARY SOURCES

1. Editions

a. Chronicles

Crónicas de los reyes de Castilla. In *Colección de las crónicas y memorias de los reyes de Castilla,* edited by Eugenio Llaguno y Amírola. Madrid: Sancha, 1779–80.

Crónicas de los reyes de Castilla. Edited by Cayetano Rosell y López. BAE, vols. 66, 68. 2 Vols. Madrid: Rivadeneyra, 1875–77. Reproduction of Llaguno y Amírola.

Las muertes del Rey don Pedro. Edited by Dionisio Ridruejo. Madrid: Alianza, 1971. Selections of the more dramatic episodes from the chronicle of Pedro I, organized to emphasize the theme of death.

Las crónicas. Edited by Cherrie L. Soper. Zaragoza: Ebro, 1975. Anthology of selections. The introduction contains useful information about Ayala's life and works.

Coronica del rey don Pedro. Edited by Constance L. Wilkins and Heanon M. Wilkins. Madison: Hispanic Seminary of Medieval Studies, 1985.

b. Libro de la caza de las aves

Libro de la caza de las aves. Translated by José Fradejas Lebrero. Valencia: Castalia, 1969.

c. Rimado de Palacio

"Libro de Poemas" o "Rimado de Palacio." Edited by Michel Garcia. 2 vols. Madrid: Gredos, 1978.

Libro Rimado del Palacio. Edited by Jacques Joset. 2 vols. Madrid: Alhambra, 1978.

Poesías del Canciller Pero López de Ayala. Edited by Albert F. Kuersteiner. Bibliotheca Hispanica, vols. 21–22. 2 vols. New York: Hispanic Society of America, 1920.

Rimado de Palacio. Edited by Florencio Janer. In *Poetas castellanos anteriores al siglo XV.* BAE, vol. 57. Madrid: Rivadeneyra, 1864, 425–76.

Rimado de Palacio. Edited by Kenneth Adams. Salamanca: Anaya, 1971. Selections. A well-balanced presentation of the biography and works of Ayala in the introduction.

Rimado de Palacio. Edited by Germán Orduna. Collana di Testi e Studi Ispanici, Testi Critici, vol. 1. 2 vols. Pisa: Giardini, 1981.

d. Theme of Job

Las Flores de los "Morales sobre Job." Edited by Francesco Branciforti. Florence: Monnier, 1963.

El Libro de Job. Edited by Francesco Branciforti. Messina: G. d'Anna, 1962.

2. Other Works

General Estoria de Alfonso el Sabio. Part 1. Edited by Antonio G. Solalinde. Madrid: Centro de Estudios Históricos, 1930.

General Estoria de Alfonso el Sabio Part 2. Edited by Antonio G. Solalinde, Lloyd A. Kasten, and Victor R. B. Oelschlager. 2 vols. Madrid: CSIC, 1957–61.

Pérez de Guzmán, Fernán. *Generaciones y semblanzas.* Edited by Robert B. Tate. London: Tamesis Books, 1965.

SECONDARY SOURCES

Alonso, Dámaso. "Tres poetas en desamparo." In *De los siglos oscuros al de Oro.* Madrid: Gredos, 1958, 114–24. Description of the reactions of three imprisoned poets: Juan Ruiz, Luis de León, and Ayala. A sensitive and artistic description of how each poet invokes the aid of the Virgin Mary.

Altamira, Rafael de. *A History of Spain.* New York: D. Van Nostrand Co., 1949.

Blanco Aguinaga, Carlos; Rodríguez Puértolas, Julio; and Zavala, Iris M. *Historia social de la literature española (en lengua castellana).* Vol. 1. Madrid: Castalia, 1979, 94–98, 110–12.

Bohigas, Pedro. "La visión de Alfonso X y Las profecías de Merlín." *Revista de filología española* 25 (1941):383–98. Refers to the prophecy concerning the succession of the Trastámaras to the Spanish throne.

Catalán, Diego. "Poesía y novela en la historiografía castellana de los siglos XIII y XIV." In *Mélanges offerts à Rita Lejeune.* Vol. 1. Gembloux: J. Duculot, 1969, 423–41.

———. *Un prosista anónimo del siglo XIV.* La Laguna: Universidad de La Laguna, 1955.

Coy, José Luis. "El *Rimado de Palacio,* las *Flores de los 'Morales sobre Job'* y una traducción atribuida al Canciller Ayala." *South Atlantic Bulletin,* 1977, 53–61. Demonstrates an obvious similarity of the three works, concluding that Ayala did the translations. Coy has several other articles dealing mainly with textual problems in these two works.

————. "Para la cronología de las obras del Canciller Ayala: la fecha de la traducción de los *Morales* de San Gregorio." *Romance Notes* 18, no. 1 (1977):141–45. Suggests that the *Morales* were written during the period 1370–80 and not in Ayala's later years. The arguments are convincing but not conclusive.

Deyermond, Alan. *Historia de la literatura española: La Edad Media.* 4th ed. Barcelona: Ariel, 1978, 215–19, 259, 265–66. An expanded and translated version of *A Literary History of Spain: The Middle Ages* (London: Ernest Benn, 1971).

————. *Historia y crítica de la literatura española.* Vol. 1, *La Edad Media,* edited by Francisco Rico. Barcelona: Crítica, 1980, 250–54, 410–13. An excellent reference tool. The text contains selections from articles and studies that aim to represent the best and most original criticism and research in Spanish medieval literature. Each chapter presents as an introduction a historical review and bibliography of the authors and works as well as a review of the present status of criticism.

Díaz Martín, Luis Vicente. *Itinerario de Pedro I de Castilla. Estudio y regesta.* Valladolid: University of Valladolid, 1975.

Díez Borque, José María, and Bordonada, A. Ena. "La prosa en la Edad Media." In *Historia de la literatura española.* Vol. 1, *Edad Media y Renacimiento,* edited by J. M. Díez Borque. Madrid: Guadiana, 1975, 377–85; 2d ed. *La Edad Media.* Madrid: Taurus, 1980, 150–59.

Díez-Echarri, Emiliano, and Franquesa, José María. *Historia de la literatura española e hispanoamericana.* 2d ed. Madrid: Aguilar, 1968, 92, 109–11.

Ferreiro Alemparte, Jaime. "Contribución documental en apoyo de la veracidad de la *Crónica del Rey Don Pedro,* del Canciller P. López de Ayala." *Ibero-romania* 3 (1971):205–12. The critic bases his enthusiasm and support for Ayala's veracity and objectivity on little documentary evidence—a will that indicates that Pedro I ordered the deaths of two men.

Floranes, Rafael. *Vida literaria del Canciller mayor de Castilla don Pedro López de Ayala restaurador de las letras en Castilla.* Colección de Documentos Inéditos para la Historia de España, vols. 19–20. 1851–52. Reprint. Millwood, N.Y.: Kraus, 1966.

Garcia, Michel. *Obra y personalidad del Canciller Ayala.* Estudios, vol. 18. Madrid: Alhambra, 1983. Abridged translation of a 1980 dissertation.

Gimeno Casalduero, Joaquín. *La imagen del monarca en la Castilla del siglo XV.* Madrid: Revista de Occidente, 1972.

————. "Pero López de Ayala y el cambio poético de Castilla a comienzos del XV." *Hispanic Review* 33 (1965):1–14. Shows the contrasting poetic styles: the traditional style of Ayala with his moral preoccupations and the new school of poetry with its emphasis on more transcendental themes and abstract ideas.

———. "La personalidad del canciller Pero López de Ayala." In *Estructura y diseño en la literatura castellana medieval.* Madrid: Porrúa, 1975, 143–63. Interesting analysis of the tragic atmosphere that Ayala maintains in the *Crónica* of Pedro I.

———. "La profecía medieval en la literatura castellana y sus relaciones con las corrientes proféticas europeas." *Nueva revista de filología hispánica* 20 (1971):64–89. Reprint in *Estructura y diseño,* 103–41.

———. "Sobre la 'oración narrativa' medieval: Estructura, origen y supervivencia." *Anales de la Universidad de Murcia, Filosofía y Letras* 16 (1957–58):113–25. Reprint in *Estructura y diseño,* 1975, 11–29.

Hillgarth, J. N. *The Spanish Kingdoms, 1250–1516.* 2 vols. Oxford: Clarendon Press, 1976–78.

Joset, Jacques. "El vocabulario poético-literario de Pero López de Ayala en el *Libro rimado del palaçio.*" In *Actas del Sexto Congreso Internacional de Hispanistas.* Toronto: University of Toronto, Department of Spanish and Portuguese, 1980, 406–10.

Kinkade, Richard P. "On Dating the *Rimado de Palacio.*" *Kentucky Romance Quarterly* 18, no. 1 (1971):17–36. A careful reading and analysis of the internal evidence in the *Rimado,* concluding that the *Rimado* as a *cancionero* has two dates of composition, 1367 and 1403.

———. "Pero López de Ayala and the Order of St. Jerome." *Symposium* 26, no. 2 (1972):161–80. Interesting article on the influence of the Order of St. Jerome on Ayala's literary works. Includes general information about the orders and their sponsors.

Lapesa, Rafael. "El Canciller P. López de Ayala y otros poetas del mester de clerecía." In *Historia general de las literaturas hispánicas,* edited by Guillermo Díaz Plaja. Vol. 1. Barcelona: Barna, 1949, 493–512. Useful and scholarly discussion. The background information is well organized and pertinent to the topic.

Lomax, Derek. *The Reconquest of Spain.* London: Longman, 1978.

Lozoya, Marqués de. *Introducción a la biografía del Canciller Ayala.* 2d ed. enl. Bilbao: Junta de Cultura de Vizcaya, 1972.

Mackay, Angus. *Spain in the Middle Ages: From Frontier to Empire 1000–1500.* London: Macmillan, 1977.

Maravall, José Antonio. *El concepto de España en la Edad Media.* Madrid: Instituto de Estudios Políticos, 1954.

Menéndez y Pelayo, Marcelino. *Historia de la poesía castellana en la Edad Media.* 2 vols. Madrid: V. Suárez, 1911–16.

Meregalli, Franco. *La vida política del Canciller Ayala.* Milan: Cisalpino, 1955.

Mérimée, Prosper. *Histoire de Don Pèdre I roi de Castille.* Paris: Librairie Marcel Didier, 1961.

Mirrer-Singer, Louise. *The Language of Evaluation: A Sociolinguistic Approach to the Story of Pedro el Cruel in Ballad and Chronicle.* Purdue University Monographs in Romance Languages, vol. 20. Amsterdam: John Benjamins, 1986.

Nader, Helen. *The Mendoza Family in the Spanish Renaissance 1350 to 1550.* New Brunswick, N.J.: Rutgers University Press, 1979, 56–76.

O'Callaghan, Joseph F. *A History of Medieval Spain.* Ithaca: Cornell University Press, 1975.

Orduna, Germán. "El fragmento P del *Rimado de Palacio* y un continuador anónimo del Canciller Ayala." *Filología* 7 (1961):107–19. Orduna suggests that 12 *octavas* in fragment P of the *Rimado* were written by an anonymous successor to Ayala and argues that the tone and point of view are not Ayala's.

Río, Angel del. *Historia de la literatura española.* Rev. ed. Vol. 1. New York: Holt, Rinehart & Winston, 1963, 113–18. Del Río talks about the modernity of Ayala as a historian. His comments about the dramatic elements in the chronicles are pertinent.

Russell, P. E. *The English Intervention in Spain and Portugal in the Time of Edward III and Richard II.* Oxford: Clarendon Press, 1955, 18–19. On the reliability of the chronicles.

————. "The *Memorias* of Fernán Alvarez de Albornoz, Archbishop of Seville, 1371–80." In *Hispanic Studies in Honour of I. González Llubera,* edited by Frank Pierce. Oxford: Dolphin, 1959, 319–29.

————. "La oración de Doña Jimena (*Poema de Mio Cid,* vv. 325–67)." In *Temas de "La Celestina" y otros estudios: Del "Cid" al "Quijote."* Letras e Ideas, Maior, vol. 14. Barcelona: Ariel, 1978, 113–58.

Salvador Miguel, Nicasio. "El Canciller Ayala y su *Rimado de Palacio.*" In *Historia de la literatura española.* Vol. 1, *Edad Media y Renacimiento,* edited by José María Díez Borque. Madrid: Guadiana, 1975, 172–78; 2d ed. *La Edad Media.* Madrid: Taurus, 1980, 445–51.

Sánchez-Albornoz, Claudio. "El canciller Ayala, historiador." *Humanitas* (Tucumán) 1, no. 2 (1953):13–46. Reprint. *Españoles ante la historia.* Buenos Aires: Losada, 1969, 99–136.

————. *Spain: A Historical Enigma.* Translated by Colette Joly Dees and David Sven Reher. 2 vols. Madrid: Fundación Universitaria Española, 1975.

Sánchez Alonso, Benito. *Historia de la historiografía española.* 2d ed. Madrid: CSIC, 1947, 1:296–302.

Sears, H. L. "The *Rimado de Palacio* and the *De Regimine Principum* Tradition of the Middle Ages." *Hispanic Review* 20 (1952):1–27.

Informative and well-organized article on Ayala's access to and use of the treatises on the governance of rulers.

Sitges, Juan Bautista. *Las mugeres del rey don Pedro I de Castilla.* Madrid: Rivadeneyra, 1910.

Strong, E. B. "The *Rimado de Palacio:* Aspects of López de Ayala's Narrative Style." *Forum for Modern Language Studies* 22, no. 1 (1986):53–61.

————. "The *Rimado de Palacio:* López de Ayala's Rimed Confession." *Hispanic Review* 37 (1969):439–51. Careful and perceptive analysis of the form and structure of the *Rimado.* Suggests that a possible source for the *Rimado* is the *Libro de la justiçia de la vida espiritual.*

————. "The *Rimado de Palacio:* López de Ayala's Satire of the Merchant Class." *Romanistisches Jahrbuch* 29 (1978):249–53.

————. "The *Rimado de Palacio:* Pero López de Ayala's Proposals for Ending the Great Schism." *Bulletin of Hispanic Studies* 38 (1961):64–77.

Suárez Fernández, Luis. *El Canciller Pedro López de Ayala y su tiempo (1332–1407).* Vitoria: Diputación Foral de Alava, 1962. A discourse delivered in Ayala's home area. Anti-Pedro I and pro-Ayala.

————. *Castilla, el cisma y la crisis conciliar.* Madrid: CSIC, 1960.

————. *Historia de España antigua y media.* 2 vols. Madrid: Rialp, 1976.

————. *Historia del reinado de Juan I de Castilla.* Vol. 1. *Estudio.* Madrid: Universidad Autónoma, 1977.

————. *Juan I, rey de Castilla (1379–1390).* Madrid: Revista de Occidente, 1955.

————. *Nobleza y monarquía: Puntos de vista sobre la historia política castellana del siglo XV.* Valladolid: Universidad, 1959; 2d ed. Valladolid: Universidad, 1975.

Tate, Robert Brian. "López de Ayala, Humanist Historian?" *Hispanic Review* 25 (1957):157–74. Reprint (in Spanish). *Ensayos sobre la historiografía peninsular del siglo XV.* Madrid: Gredos, 1970, 33–54. Thorough and enlightening discussion of Ayala as a humanist historian. Considers some of the literary sources used by Ayala in the *Crónicas.*

Urrutia, Louis. "Algunas observaciones sobre el libro por muchos mal llamado *Rimado de Palacio.*" *Cuadernos Hispanoamericanos* 238–40 (October–December 1969):459–74. Discusses the structure and main topics of the *Rimado.* Concludes that more investigations should be made on all of Ayala's works.

Valbuena Prat, Angel. *Historia de la literatura española.* 7th ed. Vol. 1. Barcelona: Gili, 1963, 187–202. The chapter on Ayala contains an interesting discussion of the literary and historical value of the *Crónicas.* Includes concise descriptions of each *Crónica.*

Vàrvaro, Alberto. "Pero López de Ayala: le *Crónicas.*" In *Manuale di filologia spagnola medievale.* Vol. 2, *Letteratura.* Naples: Liguori, 1969, 181–85.

Index